Anonymous

Smith's hand-book and guide in Philadelphia

Containing a general view of the city

Anonymous

Smith's hand-book and guide in Philadelphia
Containing a general view of the city

ISBN/EAN: 9783337145507

Printed in Europe, USA, Canada, Australia, Japan

Cover: Foto ©Andreas Hilbeck / pixelio.de

More available books at **www.hansebooks.com**

SMITH'S HAND-BOOK

AND

GUIDE IN PHILADELPHIA,

CONTAINING:

A GENERAL VIEW OF THE CITY; ITS GOVERNMENT, PUBLIC BUILDINGS, EDUCATIONAL, LITERARY, ECCLESIASTICAL, SCIENTIFIC, AND BENEVOLENT INSTITUTIONS; PLACES OF PUBLIC AMUSEMENTS, RAILROADS, AND ROUTES FROM, AND IN THE CITY; HOTELS, PUBLIC PARKS AND CEMETERIES.

AND A NEW MAP.

PHILADELPHIA:
GEORGE DELP & CO., PRESS BUILDING.
1871.

CONTENTS.

	Page.
Map of the City,	
GENERAL VIEW OF THE CITY,	5 and 13
Streets,	3
Buildings,	3
Population,	3
Voters,	7
Assessed Value of Real Estate, &c.,	8
Foreign Trade,	9 and 19
Manufacturing Industry,	9
United States Taxes,	12
Elective Districts,	12
Harbor,	12

MUNICIPAL GOVERNMENT.

Mayor,	16
Select and Common Council,	17
Police Department,	18
Chief of Police,	18
High Constables,	18
Detective Force,	18
Police Sations,	19
Fire Department,	20
Fire Districts,	21
Police and Fire Telegraph,	21
Water Supply,	21
The Fairmount Water Works,	22
The Schuylkill Water Works,	22
The Delaware Water Works,	23
The Twenty-Fourth Ward Water Works,	23
Reservoirs,	23

CONTENTS.

	Page.
Department of Markets,	24
Public Markets,	24
New Markets,	25
Law Department,	26
City Controller,	26
City Treasurer,	27
Department of City Railroads,	27
Department of Trusts,	27
Receiver of Taxes,	27
Board of Revision of Tax Payers,	27
Department of Surveys,	28
Department of City Property,	28
Board of Health,	28
Registration Department of the Board of Health,	29
Lazaretto,	29
City or Municipal Hospital,	29
City Gas Works,	29
Department of Highways,	31
Chief Inspector of Streets,	32
Guardians of the Poor,	32
Blockley Alms House,	33
Girard Estate,	35
Board of Building Inspectors,	35
Port Wardens,	36

Civil Courts.

United States Courts,	37
United States Marshall,	38
District Clerks United States Courts,	38
Supreme Court of the State of Pennsylvania,	38
District Court,	39
Prothonotary of District Courts,	40
Court of Common Pleas,	40
The Insolvents' Court,	40
Registers' Court,	40
Prothonotary of Court of Common Pleas,	40

CONTENTS.

	Page.
Court of Oyer and Terminer,	41
Court of Quarter Sessions,	41
The Clerk of Court of Quarter Sessions,	41
The Orphans' Court,	41
Clerk of Orphans' Court,	41
District Attorney,	41
Sheriff of the City and County,	42
City Commissioners,	42
Recorder of Deeds,	42
Register of Wills,	42
The Coroner,	42
Justices of the Peace,	43
The Recorder,	43
Aldermen,	43
Police Magistrates,	43
Constables,	43
Elections,	44

THE PENNSYLVANIA PRISON SYSTEM.

Prison Society of Philadelphia,	46
State Penitentiary,	47
The Moyamensing Prison,	49
House of Refuge,	50

PUBLIC BUILDINGS, AND COMMERCIAL BUILDINGS AND INSTITUTIONS.

State House,	52
Navy Yard,	54
United States Arsenal, Frankford,	54
United States Arsenal, Gray's Ferry Road,	54
United States Naval Asylum,	55
United States Mint,	55
Postal Arrangements,	56
United States Mail Stations,	56
Custom House,	57

viii   CONTENTS.

	Page
Custom House Officers,	58
Naval Officer and Clerks,	58
Storekeeper of Customs,	58
Surveyor of the Port,	58
Inspectors of Customs,	58
Appraiser's Office,	58
Weighers, Gaugers and Measurers,	59
Assistant Treasurer of United States,	59
Banks,	59
Bank Clearing House,	62
Saving Fund Societies,	63
Insurance Companies,	63
Philadelphia Board of Trade,	63
Philadelphia Corn Exchange,	64
Philadelphia Exchange Building,	64
The Board of Brokers,	64
The Commercial Association,	65
Bridges,	65
City Tobacco Warehouse,	66
City Armory,	66

EDUCATION.

Public Schools,	67
Board of Controllers of Public Schools,	67
Board of Directors of Public Schools,	67
Central High School,	68
Girls' High and Normal School,	68
Girard College,	68
Board of Directors of Girard College,	69
Officers of Girard College,	69
University of Pennsylvania,	70
Medical Colleges,	70
Jefferson Medical College,	71
The Philadelphia University,	71
Medicine and Surgery,	71

CONTENTS.   ix

	Page
Eclectic Medical College,	71
Medical Society of Pennsylvania,	71
American Medical Association,	71
College of Physicians,	71
Northern Medical Association of the State of Pennsylvania,	71
Homeopathic Medical College of Pennsylvania,	72
Female Medical College,	72
College of Dental Surgery,	72
Philadelphia Dental College,	72
College of Pharmacy,	72
Alumni Association.	72
County Medical Society,	72
Theological Schools,	72
Educational Associations,	74
Hebrew Education Society,	74
Polytechnic College,	74
Institute for Colored Youths,	74
Association of Friends for free Instruction,	74
Board of Education of the Presbyterian Church,	74
Baptist Educational Society,	74
Training School for Feeble-minded Children,	75
Institution for the Instruction of the Blind,	75
Home of Industry for the Blind,	76
Institution for the Deaf and Dumb,	76

LITERARY AND SCIENTIFIC ASSOCIATIONS.

American Philosophical Society,	78
Historical Society,	79
Academy of Natural Sciences,	80
Horticultural Society,	82
Athenæum,	82
The Franklin Institute,	83
Agricultural Society,	83
Philadelphia Lyceum,	84

CONTENTS.

	Page.
Philadelphia City Institute,	84
Spring Garden Institute,	84
Kensington Institute,	84
Moyamensing Institute,	84
West Philadelphia Institute,	84
Wagner Free Institute,	84

FINE ARTS.

Pennsylvania Academy of Fine Arts,	85
Engravers,	86
Photographers' Association,	86
Institution for the Encouragement of Apprentices and Amateurs in Works of Ingenuity and Design,	86
School of Design for Women,	87
Graphic Association,	87
Artist Fund Society,	87
Numismatic Society,	87

LIBRARIES.

Library Company of Philadelphia,	88
Mercantile Library,	90
Library of the Franklin Institute,	90
German Library,	91
Library of the Pennsylvania Hospital,	91
Apprentices' Library,	91
Friends' Free Library,	91
Law Library,	92
Library Association of 23d Ward,	92
Presbyterian Historical Library,	92
Southwark Library,	92
Girard Library,	92
Library Association of Friends,	92
Library of University of Pennsylvania,	70
Library of Academy of Natural Sciences,	80
Athenæum Library,	82

CONTENTS.

	Page.
Library of Historical Society,	79
Library of Academy of Fine Arts,	85
Library of Horticultural Society,	82
Library of Pennsylvania Hospital,	110

CHURCHES.

Swedes' Church,	94
Friends' Meeting Houses,	94
Episcopal Churches,	96
Baptist Churches,	98
Presbyterian Churches,	99
Dutch Reformed Chnrch,	103
Moravian Church,	103
New Jerusalem Church,	103
Lutheran Church,	103
German Reformed,	103
Roman Catholic Churches,	104
Methodist Churches,	105
Hebrew Synagogues,	105
Independent Churches,	106
Christian Churches,	106
Bible Christian Churches,	106
Disciples of Christ,	106
Church of the New Testament,	106
Mariners' Churches,	106
Evangelical Association,	106
German Baptists,	106
Unitarian Churches,	106
Universalists Churches,	106
Congregationalist Churches,	106
French Evangelist Churches,	106
Spiritualist Churches,	106
Missionary Boards,	107
Bible and Tract Publication Societies,	108
Board of Education,	109

CONTENTS.

BENEVOLENT INSTITUTIONS.

	Page
Pennsylvania Hospital,	110
Pennsylvania Hospital for the Insane.	111
Will's Hospital for the Blind and Lame,	112
Hospital of the Protestant Episcopal Church,	113
Charity Hospital,	113
St. Joseph's Hospital,	113
The Children's Hospital of Philadelphia, (Blight street,)	113
Howard Hospital and Infirmary,	114
Philadelphia Lying-in Charity and Nurse Society,	114
German Hospital,	114
Preston Retreat,	114
St. Francis' Hospital,	114
Jews' Hospital,	114
Christ Church Hospital,	115
The City, or Municipal Hospital,	116
City Hospital, (Blockley)	116
Women's Hospital,	116
The Homeopathic Infirmary,	116
Children's Hospital, (11th street,)	116
Dispensaries,	116
Magdalen Asylum,	118
House of the Good Shepherd,	118
Rosine Association,	118
Philadelphia Orphans' Asylum,	118
Widows' and Single Women's Society,	118
Asylum for Persons deprived of their Reason,	119
Burd Asylum,	119
The Penn Asylum for Widows,	119
Asylum for Orphans and Widows of the Lutheran Church,	119
St. John's Asylum for Orphan Boys,	119
St. Joseph's Female Orphan Asylum,	119
St. Vincent's Orphans' Asylum,	119

CONTENTS. xiii

	Page
St. Ann's Widows' Asylum,	119
German Reformed Orphan Asylum,	119
Colored Orphans' Asylum,	119
The Northern Home for Friendless Children,	120
Children's Home,	120
The Western Provident Home Association,	120
The Temporary Home Association,	120
The Newsboys' Aid Society,	120
Industrial Home for Girls,	121
Home for Destitute Colored Children,	121
Foster Home Association,	121
Association for Moral Reform of Destitute Children,	121
The Grandom Institution,	121
Lutheran Home for Orphans,	122
St. Vincent's Home for Infants,	122
Church Home for Children,	122
Howard Institution,	122
Young Men's Home of Philadelphia,	122
Female Society of Philadelphia,	122
The Provident Society,	122
Union Benevolent Society,	122
Western Association for Relief of the Poor,	122
The Northern Association for the Relief of the Poor,	123
The Central Employment Association,	123
The Philadelphia Employment Association,	123
The Home Missionary Society,	123
United Hebrew Relief Association,	123
Association of Friends for the Relief of the Poor,	123
Female Association for the Relief of the Sick,	123
The Philadelphia Association for the Relief of Disabled Firemen,	123
Soup Houses,	123

MISCELLANEOUS ASSOCIATIONS.

The Masonic Order,	124
Independent Order of Odd Fellows,	124

	Page
Sons of Temperance,	125
Society of the Sons of St. George,	125
Albion Society,	125
Hibernian Society,	125
St. Andrew's Society,	125
Scots Thistle Society,	125
French Society,	125
German Society,	125
The Welsh Society,	126
Swiss Society,	126
Union League,	126
Union League House,	126
National Union Club,	128
The Press Club,	128
United American Mechanics,	129
Pennsylvania Club,	129
Keystone Club,	129
Philadelphia Club,	129
Boat Clubs,	129

EXCHANGE AND BUSINESS ASSOCIATIONS.

Board of Brokers of People's Exchange,	129
Butchers' and Melters' Association,	129
Coal Exchange of Philadelphia,	129
Farmers' Hay Exchange,	129
Philadelphia Drug Exchange,	129
FOREIGN CONSULS IN PHILADELPHIA,	130

PLACES OF AMUSEMENT.

Theatres,	133
Academy of Music,	134
Walnut Street Theatre,	133 and 136
Arch Street Theatre,	136
Chestnut Street Theatre,	137
Fox's New American Theatre,	137

CONTENTS. XV

	Page.
Carncross and Dixey's Ethiopian Opera,	137
Concert Hall,	137
Philadelphia Museum,	137
Assembly Buildings,	137
Musical Fund Hall,	137
Handel and Haydn Hall,	137
Skating Parks,	138

PUBLIC SQUARES AND PARKS.

State House, or Independence Square,	139
Washington Square,	140
Franklin Square,	140
Logan Square,	140
Rittenhouse Square,	140
Penn Squares,	141
Jefferson Square,	141
Norris Square,	141
Shackamaxon Square,	141
Hunting Park,	141
Parade Ground,	142
Fox Square,	142
Germantown Square,	142
Fairmount Park,	142
Lansdowne Park,	143
Point Breeze Park and Race Course,	143

CEMETERIES.

Swedes' Church Burial Ground,	144
Friends' Burial Ground,	144
Christ Church Burial Ground,	144
The Mutual Burial Ground,	145
Laurel Hill Cemetery,	145

CONTENTS.

	Page
Woodland Cemetery,	145
Ronaldson Cemetery,	145
Machpelah Cemetery,	145
Lebanon Cemetery,	145
Philadelphia Cemetery,	146
Philanthropic Cemetery,	146
Lafayette Cemetery,	146
Cathedral Cemetery,	146
Glenwood Cemetery,	146
Mount Vernon Cemetery,	146
Monument Cemetery,	146
Odd Fellows' Cemetery.	146
American Mechanics' Cemetery,	146
St. Mary's Cemetery,	146
Olive Cemetery,	146
Mount Moriah Cemetery,	146
Mount Sinai Cemetery,	146
Friends' Cemetery,	146
Fair Hill Cemetery,	146
Hebrew Cemetery,	146
Cedar Hill Cemetery,	146
Leverington Cemetery,	147
Beth-el-Emeth Cemetery,	147
Potters' Field,	147

HOTELS.

Continental Hotel,	148
Girard House,	148
La Pierre House,	148
Merchant's Hotel,	149
American Hotel,	149
Washington House,	149
Bingham House,	149
Union Hotel,	149

	Page
Bald Eagle Hotel,	149
Barley Sheaf,	149
St. Lawrence Hotel,	149
Allegheny,	149
Arch Street House,	149
Markoe House,	149
St. Charles Hotel,	149
Mount Vernon Hotel,	150
Ridgeway House,	150
We tern Hotel,	150
Walnut Street House,	150

NEWSPAPERS.

First Newspaper Published in Philadelphia,	151
Press of Philadelphia	152
Daily Newspapers,	152
Tri-Weekly,	153
Weekly,	153
Periodicals,	155

RAIL ROADS.

Pennsylvania Central Railroad,	159
Philadelphia and Reading Railroad,	162
New York Lines,	165
Camden and Amboy Railroad, *via* South Amboy.,	165
Camden and Amboy Railroad, *via* Jersey City,	165
New York, Philadelphia and Trenton Railroad, *via* Kensington,	166
Raritan and Delaware Bay Railroad for New York,	166

	Page.
Camden and Atlantic Railroad,	167
West Jersey Railroad for Cape May,	167
Philadelphia, Wilmington and Baltimore Railroad,	168
Philadelphia, Germantown and Norristown Railroad, Germantown Branch,	169
Norristown Branch,	169
West Chester Railroad,	169
Pennsylvania and Erie Railroad,	170
North Pennsylvania Railroad,	171

CITY PASSENGER RAIL ROADS.

Second and Third Street Railway,	172
Green and Coates Street Railway,	172
Germantown Passenger Railway,	172
Frankford and Southwark Railway,	173
Union Passenger Railway,	173
Fairmount Branch, *Union Line*,	173
Tenth and Eleventh Street, or Citizens' Passenger Railway,	174
Thirteenth and Fifteenth Street Railway,	174
Seventeenth and Nineteenth Street Railway,	174
Richmond and Schuylkill, or Girard Avenue Railway,	174
Ridge Avenue and Manayunk Passenger Railway,	174
Fairmount and Exchange, or Race and Vine Street Railway,	175
Hestonville, Mantua and Fairmount Passenger Railway,	175
West Philadelphia, Market Street Railway,	175
Darby Passenger Railway,	175
Philadelphia City Passenger Railway,	175
Philadelphia and Gray's Ferry—Spruce and Pine Street Passenger Railway,	175
Philadelphia and Olney Railway,	176
North Philadelphia Railway,	176
Delaware County Railway,	176

CONTENTS.

	Page.
Lombard and South Street Railway,	176

FERRIES.

West Jersey Ferry,	177
Camden and Philadelphia Ferry,	177
Camden Ferry,	177
Cooper's Point Ferry,	177
Gloucester Ferry,	177
Red Bank Ferry,	177
Steamboats Plying on the Delaware,	177

MISCELLANEOUS.

Rates of Fare, &c., of Hackney Coaches,	179
Telegraph Companies,	181
United States Assessors,	182
United States Collectors of Taxes,	182
Revenue Agency,	182
Military Organizations,	183
Officers of United States Army in Philadelphia,	183
United States Quartermaster,	183
United States Pay Department,	183
United States Subsistence Department,	184
Commanding Officer Post of Philadelphia,	184
Assistant Surgeon United States Army,	194
United States Hospital,	184
United States Pension Agency,	184
State Militia,	184
National Guards' Hall,	185
Philadelphia Volunteer Refreshment Saloons,	186
Volunteers to the United States Army from Philadelphia,	186
Bounties Contributed and Paid by Philadelphia to Volunteers,	186
Contributions to Families of Volunteers,	186
Appropriations for Local Defence,	186

xx CONTENTS.

	Page.
Cooper's Shop Volunteer Refreshment Saloon,	187
Union Volunteer Refreshment Soloon,	188
Commerce of Philadelphia,	190
Philadelphia the Manufacturing Metropolis of the Union.	192

MERCHANTS' EXCHANGE, Dock Street and Walnut

PHILADELPHIA.

A GENERAL VIEW OF THE CITY.

Though ranking as the second in population, Philadelphia is beyond question the largest city in the number of buildings, extent of paved streets, and manufacturing industry in America.

It was founded in 1682 by William Penn, and incorporated in 1701. The bounds of the city were then declared to be from the river Delaware on the east, to the river Schuylkill on the west; and from Vine street on the north, to Cedar or South street on the south. The population of the city rapidly extended beyond these boundaries. The suburbs were subsequently incorporated into districts, thus forming ten or twelve governments for what was properly but one city. The inconvenience of this arrangement, long obvious, existed until 1854. In that year the various districts were consolidated into one municipal government.

The jurisdiction of the city now extends over the entire county of Philadelphia, in like manner as New York city embraces the entire county of New York.

The city area, now planned with street grades and lines, extends from the "Point House" on the south to a line on the north, including Germantown, Chestnut Hill, Manayunk and Frankford; and from the Delaware river to a distance of about two miles west of the Schuylkill river.

Within this prescribed area there is about three hundred (300) miles of paved streets, and over one hundred and eleven thousand buildings (111,000). No account is taken of buildings in the rural districts. The population is now computed at nearly eight hundred thousand (800,000). If the so-called "floating population" is included, it would far exceed these figures. In 1840 the population was 258,000; in 1850 it was 440,000; in 1860 it was 565,529. The rapid increase of the city can be realized when we state that the portion of the city north of Callowhill street, and west of Ridge avenue, with the exception of a few buildings on Coates' street, and about one hundred and fifty in Francisville, were "Commons" in 1850.

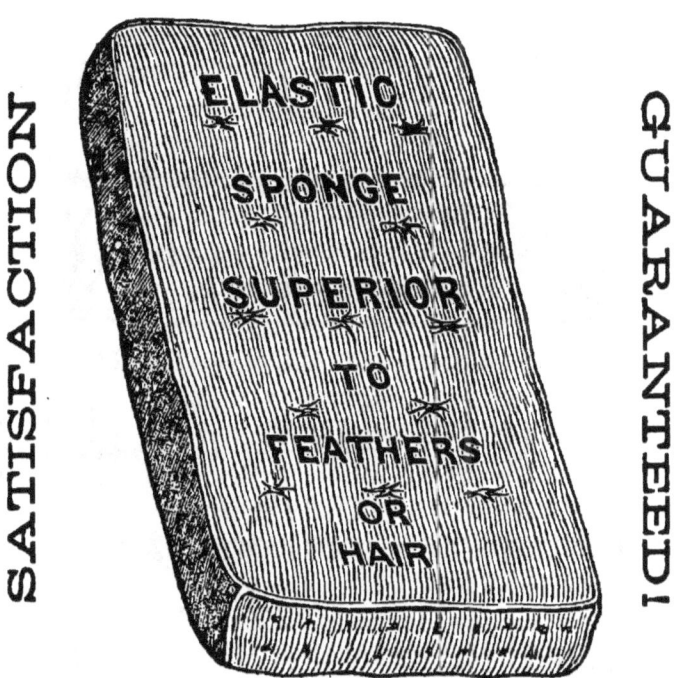

ELASTIC SPONGE, as a substitute for curled hair for all upholstery purposes, is much cheaper than feathers or hair, and far superior. Physicians universally recommend it as the dryest, cleanest and most healthful bedding known.

It will not mat or pack at all; is always free from insect life, and if soiled in any way, can be renovated more readily than any other mattress.

Special attention given to furnishing churches, halls, cars, &c.; and as it will not burn, has also this great additional advantage for railroad and sleeping car purposes, as fire can be smothered out with it.

Every article made of the ELASTIC SPONGE is guaranteed to give satisfaction.

For sale by all the principal Furniture Dealers and Upholsterers.

PENN'A ELASTIC SPONGE CO.

No. 1111 CHESTNUT STREET, PHILADELPHIA.

WHOLESALE AND RETAIL DEALERS:

PENN'A ELASTIC SPONGE COMPANY, 1111 Chestnut Street.
JOSEPH WALTON & CO., Furniture Dealers, 413 Walnut St.
P. P. GUSTINE, Furniture Dealer, Second and Race Streets.
AMOS HILLBURN, Upholsterer, 44 North Tenth Street.
BELL & CO., Furniture Dealers, 223 North Sixth Street.
RICHMOND & CO., Furniture Dealers, 45 South Second Street.

M. WALKER & SONS,

MANUFACTURERS OF

WIRE and CORRUGATED
Wrought Iron Railing

SUITABLE FOR ENCLOSING

CEMETERY LOTS, COTTAGES,

BANK COUNTERS, &c.

WROUGHT IRON FARM FENCES,

IN GREAT VARIETY FOR FENCING

Lawns, Country Seats, &c. Wire Webbing, for Poultry Yards, Ornamental Wire Work for Conservatories, Green Houses, Gardens, &c. Every variety of Wire Cloth for Paper Makers, Iron Bedsteads, Screens for Coal, Sand and Gravel.

WIRE GUARDS

FOR

STORE FRONTS, FACTORIES, ASYLUMS &c.

Every information furnished by Manufacturers,

M. WALKER & SONS,

No. 11 North Sixth Street,

PHILADELPHIA.

Receipts of cotton by water at this port for the years 1865-6:

	1865. Bales.	1866. Bales.		1865. Bales.	1866. Bales.
South America	1,406	400	New Orleans	3,596	7,079
West Indies	386	300	Mobile	196	360
Charleston	2,528	2,788	Wilmington	322	1,107
Savannah	3,532	8,465			
Total				11,966	20,517

Receipts of naval stores at this port for the years 1865-6:

	1865.	1866.
Rosin, bbls	4,136	25,298
Tar, bbls	1,041	3,513
Pitch, bbls	45	1,322
Spirits Turpentine, bbls	497	3,931
Total	5,719	34,064

To specify the various branches of productive industry in the city would far exceed the limits and scope of this work. The Iron, Coal, and Petroleum trade, each in themselves of enormous magnitude, would require a volume to do justice to this subject. There was paid to the Department of Internal Revenue of the United States by Philadelphia, during the year ending June 30th, 1864, $6,038,998; while the special income tax, levied in 1864, on the profits of business, &c., was $2,330,358, making a total of taxation levied in the city in 1864, $8,364,356, for the general government.

The city comprises 27 wards; 5 Congressional, 4 Senatorial, and 17 Representative Districts.

It commands extensive water privileges; the Delaware river, from its mouth to the city, having sufficient depth to float the largest vessels built. (In the year 1856, the ship "Cathedral" attempted to enter the harbor of New York. She was so deep in the water that she could not cross the bar. Her destination was immediately changed to Philadelphia, which port she reached without difficulty, and landed her cargo at a city wharf). The Schuylkill river, a stream in itself larger than the Thames at London, winds its way through the centre of a large portion of the city. The waters of both rivers are fresh. The air pure and the climate temperate; these with the admirable location and general plan of the city, renders it one of the most healthy in the United States.

With some few exceptions, the streets of the city cross each other at right angles; those south of Callowhill street, running nearly due north and south. The streets in the north-east portion of the city present a more irregular appearance. The plan of the city is divided by two principal streets, viz.:—High or Market street, running east and west; and Broad or 14th street, running north and south. At the intersection of these noble avenues, Penn appropriated ground—the present "Penn Squares,"—for the erection of "City Buildings." Why are not his wishes carried out?

The streets running north and south are designated in numerical order, from the Delaware river: as Front street, Second street,

Third street, and so on: while those running east and west are designated by the names of trees, &c., such as Chestnut street, Walnut street, Spruce street or Pine street, or fancy names, principally however, after some noted citizen of the country.

The city is divided north and south from Market, or High street; the cross streets south of that line are designated as south Second street, south Third street, &c. Those north are designated as north Second street, north Third street, &c.

The numbering of houses are by blocks. Thus, the block from Front to Second street, is numbered from *one* to *one hundred;* from Second to Third street from *two hundred* to *three hundred*, and so on. The convenience of this arrangement is very great; for a person desiring to find the number of say 607 Sansom street, knows that it is between 6th and 7th streets.

Railways traverse all the leading streets, upon which convenient cars run every few minutes, affording easy transit to or from any point in the city.

The general plan of Philadelphia is complete, the streets running as they mostly do for miles in a straight line, add grandeur to their appearance, while they admit a full current of air to all quarters.

THE MUNICIPAL GOVERNMENT

consists of a Mayor, a Select and Common Council.

THE MAYOR is elected by the people for a term of three years. The qualifications for this important office require the candidate to be at least thirty years of age, to be a citizen of the United States, and to have resided seven years preceding his election in the State—the last two thereof in the city.

The authority of the Mayor is complete and extensive. In addition to his other powers conferred by law, he is the Chief of the Police force. He has all the powers likewise formerly possessed by the Sheriff of the County over the military. In case of riot, he can call in the aid of that power, and it is the duty of the Major-General or commanding officer of the District to assist him promptly with such portion, or the whole of his department, as may be required.

Mayor, Daniel M. Fox.

Mayor's Office, City Hall, S. W. corner of Fifth and Chestnut streets, 2d story.

THE SELECT COUNCIL consists of twenty-six members, one from each ward. They are elected by the people for a term of three years. It is so arranged that one-third of the entire number are elected annually. The members of this board must have the same qualifications as are required by the State Constitution for members of the State Senate.

By law it is provided that each ward shall have a member of

COMMON COUNCIL for each two thousand taxable inhabitants that it contains, according to the list of taxables for the preceding year. The members of this body are elected for a term of two years, and their election is so arranged that one-half are chosen annually. The Common Council at present consist of 49 members.

The Stated Meetings of Councils are held on the Thursdays of each week, at 3 o'clock, P. M.

Council Chambers, second story of the State House. That of the Select Council in the east room, and that of the Common Council in the west room. These chambers are neatly fitted up. A visit to either will prove entertaining. The sessions are open to the public.

Council Rooms and Clerk's Office, City Hall, S. W. corner of Fifth and Chestnut streets, second story, east room.

The business of the Corporation is transacted under DEPARTMENTS, viz.:—Police, Fire, Water

Markets, Law, City Controller, City Treasurer, City Railroads, Taxes, Trusts, Health, Girard Estate, Gas, Poor, Highways, Surveys, and City Property.

THE POLICE DEPARTMENT, embraces the Mayor as Executive, the Mayor's clerks, 1 Chief of Police, 8 High Constables, 1 Chief of Detectives, 8 Detectives, 17 Lieutenants, 33 Sargeants, 663 Patrol men, 17 Police Magistrates, and 1 Fire Marshal.

The force is divided into a centre station and 16 Police Districts.

Central Police Station, City Hall, first door below Chestnut street. (S. W. cor. 5th and Chestnut.)

This is also the headquarters of the Chief of Police, the High Constables, Detectives, Reserve Corps, and Fire Marshal.

Persons arrested for felony, have a hearing at this station before the Mayor, or a Police Magistrate selected by him.

The Chief of Police holds office by appointment from the Mayor, by and with the approval of the Select Council.

The High Constables are appointed to enforce the city ordinances in relation to hackney-coaches, obstructions on streets, signs, awnings, &c.

The Detective Force are detailed for the detention and arrest of criminals, and the recovery of stolen property.

First Police District Station House—N. E. corner of Twentieth and Fitzwater streets.

Second Police District Station House—Southwark Hall, Second street above Christian street.

Third Police District Station House—Union street below Third street.

Fourth Police District Station House—Cherry street west of Fourth street.

Fifth Police District Station House—Fifteenth street above Locust street.

Sixth Police District Station House—Filbert street west of Fifteenth street.

Seventh Police District Station House—Northern Liberty Hall, Third street below Green street.

Eighth Police District Station House—Spring Garden Hall, Thirteenth and Spring Garden streets.

Ninth Police District Station House—N. W. corner Twenty-third and Brown streets.

Tenth Police District Station House—Commissioners' Hall, Front and Master street.

Eleventh Police District Station House—Dauphin street and Trenton avenue.

Twelfth Police District Station House—N. W. corner of Tenth and Thompson streets.

Thirteenth Police District Station House—Manayunk.

Fourteenth Police District Station House—Germantown Hall, Germantown.

*Fifteenth Police District Station House—*Frankford.

*Sixteenth Police District Station House—*West Philadelphia Hall, corner of Market and 39th streets.

In case of riot, the police force, by the aid of the " Police Telegraph" and city railroads, can be concentrated promptly to any point in the city.

Strangers desiring information or directions in the city, should address one of these officers, readily distinguished by their blue uniform, who are required to be, and always are courteous and obliging to those seeking information. Should they desire the aid of a police-magistrate, go direct to the Mayor's office.

THE FIRE DEPARTMENT is under the direction of a Chief Engineer, a Secretary and five Assistant Engineers.

The force consists of 89 companies, having in their possession 39 steam engines; 25 hand engines; 113 hose carriages; 7 hook and ladder trucks with 1300 feet of ladders; 154 axes; 53 hooks; 89,410 feet of hose, and 1130 feet of suction hose. There are connected with the Department 39 engineers of steam engines, 39 drivers, 80 horses, and 33 ambulances.

The total number of members, including active, honorary, and contributing is 12,724.

The city is divided into seven Fire Districts, viz.: *First District* extends from the Delaware river to the Schuylkill river, south of Spruce street.

Second Fire District, from Spruce street to Race street, and from the Delaware river to the Schuylkill river.

Third Fire District, from Race street to Green street, and from the Delaware river to the Schuylkill river.

Fourth Fire District, from Green street to Allegheny avenue, and from the Delaware river to the Schuylkill river.

Fifth Fire District, north of Allegheny avenue from Broad street to the Delaware river.

Sixth Fire District, north of Allegheny avenue from Broad street to the Schuylkill river.

Seventh Fire District, Twenty-fourth ward, or all west of the Schuylkill river.

OFFICE OF THE CHIEF ENGINEER—City Hall, S. W. corner of Fifth and Chestnut streets.

OFFICE OF THE POLICE AND FIRE TELEGRAPH—City Hall, S. W. corner of Fifth and Chestnut street, first floor, west room.

The Police and Fire Telegraph arrangements of this city are complete and perfect.

THE WATER SUPPLY of the city is derived from the Fairmount Works; Schuylkill Works; Delaware Works, and the Twenty-fourth Ward Works, all under charge of the

WATER DEPARTMENT, which consists of a Chief Engineer, a Register, a Chief Clerk, five Permit Clerks, a Messenger, four Inspectors, four Purveyors; two Engineers at Fairmount Works, two at Delaware Works, and two at the Twenty-fourth Ward Works.

THE FAIRMOUNT WORKS are situated on the east shore of the Schuylkill river, above the Suspension Bridge. Visitors to Fairmount will take the Green and Coates street, Race and Vine street, Arch street, or Seventh and Ninth street (Union line) cars, all of which lines run direct to Fairmount.

These magnificent works were erected in 1819, but have been subsequently enlarged and improved. The works are now in excellent order. They supply the 1st, 2d, 3d, 4th, 5th, 6th, 7th, 8th, 9th and 10th wards. The first four wards are supplied from the Corinthian avenue reservoir; the others from the reservoirs at Fairmount.

Fairmount has long been regarded as the pride of Philadelphia, and no stranger should leave the city without visiting it. The grounds have lately been largely extended, and they are now, in connection with "Fairmount Park," the most popular place of resort in or about the city.

THE SCHUYLKILL WATER WORKS are situated also on the same river, at the foot of Thompson street. These works supply the 11th, 12th, 13th, 14th, and 15th wards.

The Delaware Water Works are situated on the river Delaware, at the foot of Wood street in the 18th ward. They supply the 16th, 17th, 18th, 19th, and 20th wards.

The 24th Ward Water Works are situated on the Schuylkill river, opposite Fairmount Park. There is no reservoir attached to these works. The large stand-pipe, an object of considerable architectural beauty, and from which a magnificent view of the city can be obtained, operates as a reservoir and regulator of the pressure.

RESERVOIRS.

The Reservoir at Fairmount is divided into four basins having in the aggregate, a capacity of 26,896,636 gallons. A fine walk surrounds these basins, from which a charming view of the city can be had.

The Corinthian Avenue Reservoir, Corinthian avenue and Poplar street, has a capacity of 37,500,000 gallons. It is 124 feet above high water. One 48-inch main, connects this reservoir with Fairmount, and a 30-inch distributing main, supplies the wards previously mentioned.

The Schuylkill Reservoir, Twenty-sixth

and Master streets, has an elevation of 124 feet above high water. Its capacity is 9,800,000 gallons.

THE DELAWARE RESERVOIR, Lehigh avenue and Sixth street, has a storage capacity of 9,400,000 gallons, and is 117 feet above high water. The facilities of distribution from these Reservoirs is extensive, and embrace about 360 miles of street main.

DEPARTMENT OF MARKETS consists of a Commissioner, Chief Clerk, and thirteen clerks to attend to the Public Markets.

This Department has the supervision of all the public wharves and landings.

Office—S. W. corner of Fifth and **Walnut** streets.

THE PUBLIC MARKETS.

Wharton Market, Moyamensing avenue.

Washington Market, Shippen street, between Third and Fifth streets.

South Eleventh Street Market, Eleventh street from Shippen to Carpenter street.

South Second Street Market, S. Second street, from Pine to South street.

North Second Street Market, N. Second street from Coates to Poplar street.

Callowhill Street Market, Callowhill street from Fourth to Seventh streets.

Spring Garden Market, Spring Garden street, from Marshall street to Twelfth street.

Girard Avenue Market, Girard avenue.

Richmond Market, from Richmond to Salmon street, 19th Ward.

Frankford Market, Frankford.

Market stands for wagons are still continued on North and South Second street, on South street from Front to Fifth street, on Broad street, at Penn Square, on Callowhill street west from Broad street, at Broad and Coates streets, and on South street west of Broad street.

In addition to these Public Markets, there are

THE NEW MARKET HOUSES

established by private enterprise.

The facade of some of these buildings are very elegant, while their construction and general arrangement is well designed for the convenience of seller and buyer. Each of these enterprises has been entirely successful. These buildings are located as follows:

Delaware Avenue Market, Delaware avenue to Water street, and Dock to Spruce street.

Eastern Market, Fifth and Merchant streets.

Farmers' Market, Market street below Twelfth street.

Franklin Market, Market street and Twelfth street.

Western Market, Market and Sixteenth streets.

Farmers' Western Market, Twenty-first and Market streets.

Union Market, Seventeenth street above Market street.

Union Market, Second above Callowhill street.

People's Market, Pine street near Nineteenth street.

Green Hill Market, Seventeenth and Poplar streets.

Avenue Market, Ridge avenue above Broad street.

Fairmount Market, Spring Garden and Twenty-second streets.

Kater Market, South street near Sixteenth street.

Germantown Market, Germantown avenue, between School and Queen streets.

It will thus be seen that this city is well supplied with markets. Few cities can boast of better.

THE LAW DEPARTMENT of the city.—Office—Law Buildings, Fifth street below Walnut street, consists of a City Solicitor, three Assistant Solicitors and one Clerk. This department has charge of all patents, deeds, wills, leases, mortgages, contracts, bonds, notes, and other evidences of debt belonging to the city.

CITY CONTROLLER.—Office—Girard Bank Building, Third street, below Chestnut street. In this department all city accounts are audited.

The controller also countersigns all warrants drawn on the City Treasury.

CITY TREASURER,—Same building, first floor, is the custodian of all city funds.

The City Controller and City Treasurer are elected by the people for a term of three years.

THE DEPARTMENT OF CITY RAILROADS is in the charge of a Superintendent who is elected by councils for a term of one year. The City Railroad extends through Market, Broad, and Willow streets.

Office—Market street east of Fifteenth street.

DEPARTMENT OF TRUSTS consists of a Superintendent, who is elected annually by councils. He has the charge of collecting and distributing certain miscellaneous trusts bequeathed to the city for charitable purposes.

Office—Wills' Hospital, Race street, west of Eighteenth street.

DEPARTMENT OF TAXES.—Office—S. E. corner of Chestnut and Sixth streets.

The principal officer of this department is THE RECEIVER OF TAXES, who is elected by the people for a term of two years. He collects the State, County, and City Taxes. The Receiver of Taxes, together with the City Treasurer and City Commissioners, form a *Board of Revision* for tax payers, for the correction of irregularities of assessments, &c.

DEPARTMENT OF SURVEYS.—Office—Law Buildings, Fifth street below Walnut street. This Department consists of a Chief Engineer and Surveyor, two Recording Clerks, a Draughtsman, a Rodman, and twelve Surveyors and Regulators, all of whom are elected by councils for a term of five years.

THE DEPARTMENT OF CITY PROPERTY.—Office, Third street, above Spruce street, west side, has charge of all the public buildings, Court rooms, offices, Parks, Squares, &c.

The Commissioner of City Property is elected annually by councils.

BOARD OF HEALTH.

This important Department is composed of twelve members, elected for a term of three years; it being arranged that four shall be elected annually as follows: one by the Judges of the District Court; one by the Judges of the Court of Common Pleas; one by the Judges of the Supreme Court, and one by the City Councils.

The officers of the Board are a President and Secretary.

The Executive Officers of the Board are a Health Officer; Port Physician; Lazaretto Physician; Quarantine Master.

The elective officers are a Clerk; Assistant Clerk; three Registration Clerks; four Messengers; one Receiver; a Night Inspector; a Stewardess of Lazaretto, and two Measurers of wells.

THE MEETINGS OF THE BOARD are not public. They are held daily from June 1st to October 1st, at 12 o'clock, M., and weekly on Tuesdays, from October 1st to June 1st. The jurisdiction of the Board of Health is ample and complete in all matters appertaining to the health and health regulations of the city and port.

The Registration Department of the Board of Health, embrace the records of the marriages, births, and deaths within the city.

The administration of this department has ever commanded the confidence of the people, as well from the high character and ability of its members, as for their judicious and efficient management of their responsible duties.

Office, S. W. corner of Sansom and Sixth streets.

THE LAZARETTO is pleasantly situated on the banks of the Delaware, about twelve miles south of the city.

THE CITY HOSPITAL is situated corner of Hart Lane and Lamb Tavern Road, 21st Ward.

THE CITY GAS WORKS are under the control of a Board of twelve Trustees elected by the City Councils, viz.: two trustees are elected by the Select Council, and two by the Common Council, annually, for a term of three years. The Board of Trustees elect THE OFFICERS OF THE DEPARTMENT, viz.: a Chief Engineer, two Assistant Engineers, a Cashier, a Register, a Superintendent of Distribution, and a Chief Clerk.

The business of the works is transacted through six offices.

THE PRINCIPAL OFFICE, Seventh street, between Market and Chestnut streets.

BRANCH OFFICES, Spring Garden Hall, Spring Garden and Thirteenth streets, one in Germantown, one in the Twenty-fourth ward, in the West Philadelphia Hall, one in Manayunk, and one in Frankford.

The City Gas Works, comprise those in the Ninth ward at Market Street Bridge, the new works at Point Breeze in the Twenty-sixth ward, the works near Fairmount in the Fifteenth ward, and those at Manayunk.

The works at Market Street Bridge were the first established, and are extensive and complete. The area of the property occupied here, comprises seven and a half acres, with a water front of eight hundred feet. In 1850 the whole of this ground was occupied by the establishment

The works at Point Breeze, on the Passyunk Road, in the Twenty-sixth ward, went into operation on the thirteenth of December, 1854.

They embrace all the modern improvements, and are highly creditable alike to the city, the various Boards of Trustees, and particularly to Mr. John C. Cresson, the late Chief Engineer of the Department. They are justly considered "model works" in their construction, simplicity, convenience, and entire adaptation to the purpose for which they were designed. They will repay a visit.

The other two works are comparatively small.

The street mains now embrace $475\frac{3}{4}$ miles; the number of lights in use is 617,770, of which 7,422 are street lamps. The total cost of the Department for 1865, was $2,242,542 95
less 200,381 70
received from the sales of Coke, Tar, &c.

The cost of manufacturing gas at these various works, averages 2\frac{70}{100}$ per 1000 cubic feet.

Department of Highways.

The Chief Commissioner of Highways and two Assistant Commissioners constitute a Board of which the Chief is President. These officers are elected by the City Councils, annually. The Department has, in addition to these, a License Clerk, a Miscellaneous Clerk, and twenty-six District Ward Inspectors. Office, Philosophical Hall, Fifth street.

This Department has charge of all matters

appertaining to the highways of the city, such as street paving, &c., also the licensing of vehicles in the city, &c. The cleansing of the streets formerly under the jurisdiction of the Highway Department, is now under the supervision of a CHIEF INSPECTOR OF STREET CLEANING, whose duties are performed by the Mayor.

GUARDIANS OF THE POOR.—Office, 42 North Seventh street.

This Board consists of twelve members who serve for a term of three years each. They are elected as follows: On the first Monday in June of each year the Judges of the Supreme Court elect one; the Judges of the District Court elect one; the Judges of the Court of Common Pleas one, and City Councils one. The parties thus selected must be electors, and reputable citizens, residing within the city.

The Guardians have the entire administration of the department under such ordinances and regulations as may be prescribed by the city councils.

THE OFFICERS OF THE BOARD, who are elected by the Guardians on the first Monday of July, annually, consist of a *President*, a *Treasurer*, a *Secretary*, a *Clerk* and *Steward*.

The annual expenses of the department is

$337,893,48, of which $245,108,00 is expended for the support of the "Blockley Alms House," and the balance, less 7,999,48, is spent for outdoor poor."

THE "BLOCKLEY ALMS HOUSE" is situated on the west side of the Schuylkill river; entrance on the Darby Post Road. Visitors will take the Market street cars to the Darby road; thence by another line of cars running from there direct to the Alms House gate.

The Institution, very extensive and complete, occupies a commanding position. It consists of four buildings, each five hundred feet long, and three stories high, including the basement.

The eastern or principal front, is ornamented with a fine portico of six columns in the Tuscan order. On the south front is a large wellstocked and cultivated garden. An extensive play-ground for the children of the house, occupies the north front. A farm of 180 acres is also attached to the property. This farm is cultivated almost entirely by the inmates. The four buildings enclose a rectangular yard, used and occupied for the general purposes of the institution.

The population of the Alms House averages about 2500. It must not be supposed they are here in idleness; under the present excellent management, those capable, are employed in various occupations: the men as laborers, weavers, shoemakers, blacksmiths, carpenters, or in farming, gardening, carting, quarrying stone, &c.; the women in sewing or general housework.

The Institution also embraces an INSANE DEPARTMENT, the number of whose inmates is about six hundred. A successful attempt has been made lately to find employment for these unfortunates. A large number of the females are engaged in plain sewing, binding shoes, &c.; while several of the men work in the adjoining garden, with considerable skill. Economy is not the object here. The sanitary results of finding employment for the mind is of far greater importance.

THE CHILDREN'S ASYLUM contains about 200 of all ages.

The arrangement of the buildings within, are on a scale corresponding with its exterior; the men's dining-hall, on the first floor, being sufficient to accommodate five hundred persons.

Attached to the House, there is also an obstetric apartment, an extensive library, and a museum.

The whole establishment is kept in excellent order, and is an object well worth the attention of the stranger.

TRUSTEES OF GIRARD ESTATE.—Office, 19 South 5th street.

The Corporation of the City of Philadelphia are the Trustees of the Girard Estate. Councils annually elect a Superintendent and an Agent. The latter rents the Girard property, under the approval of a Committee of Councils.

BOARD OF BUILDING INSPECTORS.—Office, Philosophical Hall, Fifth street below Chestnut street, 2d story west room.

By the "Act of Assembly" of 1808, it is provided that a "Board of Building Inspectors" shall be appointed as follows:—In the month of May, one by the Judges of the Supreme Court, one by the Judges of the Court of Common Pleas, and on the third Thursday in April, one by the Common Council, for a term of three years. Vacancies supplied by the appointing power.

It is the duty of these Inspectors to visit in person, or by deputy, and inspect all buildings in progress of construction or alteration, and to see that such house, or houses, or buildings are being constructed or altered in compliance with the Laws made and provided therefor.

Permits for building are granted by this Department, and no building can be erected or altered within the "fire limits" of the city, without such a permit.

PORT WARDENS are also appointed by the Common Council. The Board consists of sixteen members, who serve for a term of two years each: eight being elected in May of each year.

THE EXECUTIVE OFFICERS comprise a Master Warden, Harbor Master, a Deputy Harbor Master and a Clerk.

The Port Wardens have jurisdiction over the harbor of Philadelphia, the construction of Docks, &c., to grant license to Pilots, and to prevent obstructions being placed in, or allowed in the harbor or in the rivers.

Office, No. 119 Walnut street.

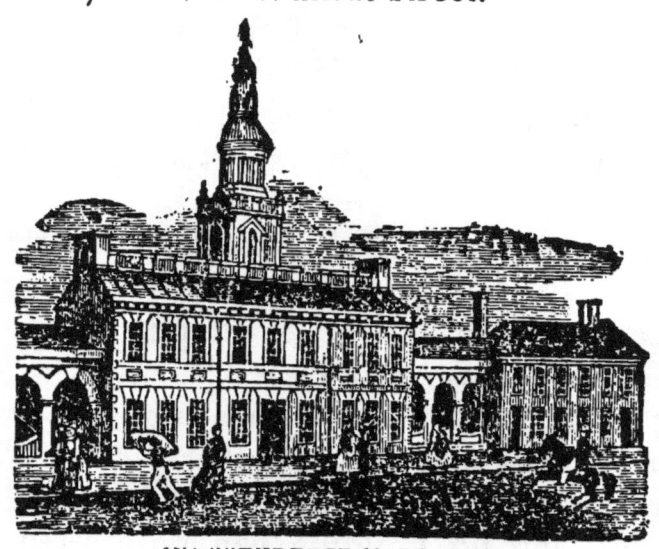

INDEPENDENCE HALL, 1776.

UNITED STATES, STATE, AND COUNTY COURTS.

CIVIL COURTS.

CIRCUIT COURT OF THE UNITED STATES, FOR THE EASTERN DISTRICT OF PENNSYLVANIA.

Court Room, Post Office Building, Chestnut street, second story. Entrance on Library street, below Fifth street.

CLERK'S OFFICE, No. 435 Library street, second story.

THE REGULAR STATED SESSIONS of this court are held on the first Monday of April, and on the first Monday of October in each year.

DISTRICT COURT OF THE UNITED STATES, FOR THE EASTERN DISTRICT OF PENNSYLVANIA.

Court Room, Post Office Building, Chestnut street. Entrance, No. 435 Library street

THE REGULAR SESSIONS of this court are held on the third Mondays of February, May, August, and November in each year.

SPECIAL SESSIONS are held for the trial of Admiralty cases.

CLERK'S OFFICE, No. 435 Library street, second story.

There is a UNITED STATES MARSHAL and six Deputy Marshals for the district. Office, No. 435 Library street, second story.

There are also two PRIZE COMMISSIONERS attached to the district.

Persons desiring affidavits taken by a United States Commissioner, can obtain the address of the various persons appointed for that purpose, by applying at the District Clerk's Office, No. 435 Library street.

SUPREME COURT
OF THE STATE OF PENNSYLVANIA.

This Court consists of one President Judge, and five Associate Judges.

COURT ROOM—East wing of State House, second story.

OFFICE OF THE PROTHONOTARY of the Supreme Court, No. 7 State House Row.

There is one term of this Court *in Banc* for the Eastern District of the State, held in Philadelphia, on the first Monday in January, and continuing thirteen weeks if required.

The other terms of the Court are held at Harrisburg, at Sunbury, and at Pittsburg.

RETURN DAYS—The first and last days of each term; the Court can fix special days.

SUPREME COURT OF PENNSYLVANIA *at Nisi Prius.*

There are three sessions of this Court held in Philadelphia, by the same Judges, alternately, commencing on the first Mondays of November, January, and March in each year.

The Judges at *Nisi Prius* hear and determine all cases in equity, brought in the Supreme Court.

RETURN DAYS—The first Monday in each month.

Judges of the Supreme Court are elected by the people for a term of fifteen years.

DISTRICT COURT—Second story of building S. E. corner of Chestnut and Sixth streets; entrance on Sixth street.

This Court consists of a President and three Associate Judges, who hold four terms in each year, commencing on the first Mondays of March, June, September and December. The Court sits *in Banc* upon the first Mondays of these months to hear motions and arguments. The Court also meets for jury trials, after the arguments have been concluded, for March, September, and December terms, which continue nine weeks for each term. There are no jury trials in the June term.

JUDGMENT DAY—The third Monday in every month.

RETURN DAY—The first Monday in each month.

The Judges of this Court are elected by the people for a term of ten years.

THE PROTHONOTARY OF DISTRICT COURT is elected by the people for a term of three years, and is paid by fees.

Office, No. 12 State House, Chestnut street.

COURT OF COMMON PLEAS consists of a President and three Associate Judges, who hold their sessions in room No. 2, State House.

The regular terms of the Court commence on the first Mondays of March and June, the third Monday in September, and the first Monday in December.

RETURN DAYS—The first Monday of each month. June Term is devoted to motions and arguments.

THE INSOLVENTS' COURT is held by the Judges of the Court of Common Pleas, four times in each year, the day being fixed by the Court. The same Judges, together with the "Register of Wills," form the REGISTER'S COURT, who hear and decide all cases in dispute before the Register of Wills.

The Judges of the Court of Common Pleas, are elected by the people for a term of ten years.

THE PROTHONOTARY OF THE COURT OF COMMON PLEAS is also elected for a term of three years, by the people. He is paid by fees.

Office, No. 9 State House, Chestnut street.

COURT OF QUARTER SESSIONS.—Chambers first floor in the building, S. E. corner of Chestnut and Sixth streets.

The Judges of the Court of Common Pleas hold a Court of Quarter Sessions six terms in each year. Road cases are also heard and disposed of by the same Judges.

They also hold a

COURT OF OYER AND TERMINER, and general jail delivery, four terms a year, at the several terms appointed for holding the Court of Quarter Sessions.

THE CLERK OF THE COURT OF QUARTER SESSIONS is elected by the people, for a term of three years. He is paid by fees.

Office, No. 10 State House, Chestnut street.

THE ORPHANS' COURT is also held by the Judges of the Court of Common Pleas. It is held the first and third Fridays of each month. There are days appropriated for hearing arguments. These Judges have also Equity and Chancery powers.

THE CLERK OF THE ORPHANS' COURT is elected by the people, for a term of three years. Paid by fees.

Office, No. 3 State House, Chestnut street.

DISTRICT ATTORNEY.—Office, No. 212 South Fifth street, second story. He is elected by the people, for a term of three years.

THE SHERIFF OF THE CITY AND COUNTY is the chief executive officer of the State and County Courts. He is elected by the people, for a term of three years, and is paid by fees.

Sheriff's Office, No. 4 State House, east wing.

CITY COMMISSIONERS.—Office, second story, room No. 11 State House. There are three of these officials. They are elected by the people, for a term of three years; one being elected annually. The City Commissioners have jurisdiction over all duties relating to assessors and assessments; to the selection and drawing of jurors, and to election and election officers.

RECORDER OF DEEDS.—Office, No. 427 Chestnut street, up stairs, is elected by the people, for three years. All deeds and mortgages on real estate, in the city and county, must be recorded in this office. Paid by fees.

REGISTER OF WILLS.—Office, No. 6 State House, east wing. All Wills must be recorded here before being acted on. He is elected by the people, for three years. Paid by fees.

THE CORONER is elected by the people, for three years. He is also paid by fees, and has jurisdiction to examine into all cases of sudden death, and as such has the power of a committing magistrate.

Office, Philosophical Hall, Fifth street, below Chestnut, first floor, front.

Justices of the Peace

In and for the City of Philadelphia, consists of a Recorder and fifty Alderman.

THE RECORDER is appointed by the Governor of the State by and with the consent of the Senate, and holds office for a term of ten years. He has all the jurisdiction and powers of a committing magistrate, equal with the Mayor, and with that officer, has charge of the city seal.

Recorder's Office, No. 521 Chestnut street.

ALDERMEN.—There are two of these officials in each ward of the city. They are elected by the people, for a term of five years, but receive their commissions from the Governor of the State. They are paid by fees.

The aldermen are committing magistrates, and have jurisdiction also in civil suits under one hundred dollars. Sixteen of these magistrates are selected by the City Councils as POLICE MAGISTRATES, viz.: one for each of the Police Districts, whose duties are to hear the charges against such parties as may be arrested by the police.

CONSTABLES.—There are two in each ward, except in the rural districts, where a larger number is allowed. Constables enter security and receive their commissions from the Court of Quarter Sessions. They are elected by the people for a term of two years, and are paid by fees.

ELECTIONS. All Congressional, State, County, and Municipal elections in this city are held on the second Tuesday in October of each year.

EASTERN PENITENTIARY, Coates street.

THE PENNSYLVANIA PRISON SYSTEM.

More earnest thought and practical effort has been devoted in Pennsylvania to education, to the alleviation of the wretchedness of the poor, and to the mental and moral diseases than in any other American community.

The founders of this State were a thinking, practical, and benevolent people, free from those excitements which zeal without knowledge often produce to degenerate into prejudice. They were christians whose faith was never carried into bigotry through emotional influences. The happiness of man, his improvement, welfare, social and moral progress, were the aims to which their exertions were directed. They had no theories of reform that were not constantly tested by practical means, as elementary to an organized system for social improvement. What they did was in obedience to conscience. Their motto of " unbroken faith" in private and public acts, was the key to their integrity of purpose, in all relation to society and government.

So far back as 1776, men of thought and action met in Philadelphia to undertake the peaceful, humane, and christian reformation of the then Colonial penal laws. This society, so early established, was the present "PHILADELPHIA SOCIETY FOR THE ALLEVIATIONS OF THE MISERIES OF PUBLIC PRISONS." The efforts of this organization resulted in the enactment of the Penal laws of 1794. This statute formed the first step in the march of enlightenment, which having attracted the attention, during its progress, of civilized nations, terminated in the present Penitentiary system of Pennsylvania.

From 1794 to 1821, the Prison Society was engaged in giving their principles a practical form. The Pennsylvania system of Penitentiary discipline was the result of their labors. At this period, the old "Walnut Street Prison," that formerly stood on the corner of Walnut and Sixth streets, was the State Prison; and the "Arch Street Prison," formerly at the corner of Broad and Arch streets, was the County Prison. In both, the convicts were mostly together, their sex only dividing them. Experience had demonstrated that this congregation of convicts, was the most cruel of all plans of punishment. The evil consequences of contamination, the bad, the unfortunate, the young offender, and the hardened in crime, the vile and irrepressible, the educated and the ignorant, combined in making a moral gangrene of the the prison population.

Separation of convicts became the next step in the progress of penitentiary reform.

Looking over, as we have been permitted to do, the labors of men engaged in this work from 1776 to 1825, we feel it due to notice, and but truth to say that the efforts of the late Roberts Vaux in behalf of the system under notice, entitle his name to rank among the first philanthropists of the age, or indeed of any age. Principally through his exertions, the Act of the Legislature of 1821, authorizing the erection of the STATE PENITENTIARY FOR THE EASTERN DISTRICT OF PENNSYLVANIA at Cherry Hill, (the designation of the ten acre farm bought for the site of the buildings; hence the name generally given the prison), was passed. The Act of 1829 reformed the penal laws of the State, and adapted them to the "separate system," to which the penitentiary was dedicated. It also enacted rules for the discipline of the prison. These two Acts are the foundation on which the Pennsylvania system rests.

In the year 1829, the first convicts were received into the new prison, those in the "Walnut Street Prison" being removed to it to serve out the terms of their respective sentences. The old prison was taken down, and the ground and materials sold, and the funds realized thereon used in furnishing the Cherry Hill Prison.

The new buildings and the ten acre farm enclosed within the walls, cost $700,000. The present value of the property, owing to the rise in real estate, is estimated at over $1,000,000. Thus the State has made a good investment. There has been 4899 prisoners confined in the penitentiary since it was opened. This small number, averaging about 334 per year, is remarkable. The "Sing Sing" Prison, in New York, has an average of inmates exceeding the whole number of convicts confined *in all the prisons in Pennsylvania.*

There are two State Prisons in this State; one at Pittsburg and the other in this city. In addition to these, there are County Prisons in Philadelphia, Montgomery, Dauphin, Berks, Lancaster, Chester, and Schuylkill counties, all built upon the "separate system."

Since the year 1825, the attention of most of the governments of Europe and America has been directed to the experimental workings of our system of prison discipline. The French authorities sent two commissioners, Messrs. Beaumont and De Toqueville, to investigate the subject in all its relations. These gentlemen on their return, published a most valuable report, in which the system is highly approved as a vast progress in penal jurisprudence. Messrs. Crawford and Newman came from Great

Britain upon a like errand; and after a careful and critical examination, a similar report was the result. From South America, several commissioners have visited our institutions. Brazil, Peru, and Chilli, have in particular, taken the liveliest interest in this effort of their northern neighbors. Indeed, we may safely say, that no social or scientific question of the age attracts more attention among civilized nations, than this.

THE STATE PENITENTIARY is situated on Coates street west of Twenty-first street. Visitors will take the Green and Coates Street Cars, (green cars.) They cross Chestnut street at Eighth street. Tickets of admission obtained from the Mayor, or Mr. Richard Vaux, No 520 Walnut street, room 3, first floor.

THE MOYAMENSING, OR PRISON OF PHILADELPHIA COUNTY. It is generally called "Moyamensing," because it is located in the District of that name, which, at the time of its erection, was a separate municipality of the old city.

This Prison, situated on Passyunk Road and Tenth street, occupies an area of about eleven acres. The "Act of Assembly" authorizing its erection was passed in 1831. The buildings were finished in 1835. It has five hundred cells, and is constructed of granite, in the Tudor or English style of Gothic architecture. The Institution is under the management of a Board of Inspectors, who are appointed by the Courts. This mode of appointment has, after various others failed, given entire satisfaction to public opinion, as the best suited for securing an efficient direction of the establishment. It receives persons charged with crime, who are unable to obtain bail for their appearance at Court for trial; disorderly and drunken persons arrested and committed for fine and costs; vagrants, and those convicted and sentenced for crime by the Philadelphia County Courts. There is a separate building attached to this prison, known as THE DEBTOR'S APARTMENT. It was erected for the reception of those who were arrested for debt by creditors. Imprisonment for debt being now abolished, this gloomy, Egyptian looking edifice is only a monument over the grave of the relics of that feudal principle which was at that time, the spirit of our inherited jurisprudence. The place is now used by the Sheriff of the County for the safe keeping of the contumacious against legal orders, or witnesses who might not be present when wanted in Court.

Visitors will take the Tenth Street cars. Tickets of admission obtained at the Mayor's office, Chestnut and Fifth streets.

HOUSE OF REFUGE—Girard avenue and Twenty-second streets. Tickets of admission obtained at 103 North Seventh street. Visitors take Ridge Avenue cars at Ninth and Arch streets to Girard avenue, thence to Refuge *via* the Girard avenue cars, and Green and Coates Street line to Twenty-first street.

Growing out of the enlightened views which had been directed to adult offenders, came the subject of the young, whether convict, outcast, vicious, or vagabond, whose neglected condition was become a serious evil. Their age, the want of proper treatment, and above all a suitable place to keep them, and their interesting relations to society, awoke efforts for their welfare.

The House of Refuge was recognized by law in the year 1826-27 as a place in which this neglected or wayward class could be reclaimed.

A voluntary association of citizens, having for its object the establishment of so needed an institution, was by Act of Assembly of the State, made a public corporation, and authorized to receive and detain juveniles committed to their custody by the Magistrates or Courts of the Commonwealth. To provide for its maintenance, appropriations are made annually from the State Treasury. Though it is not in the strict term a prison, yet it is a place of restraint, a house of detention. The inmates are educated both mentally and in handicrafts, or bound to approved good masters as apprentices.

The managers of this institution erected their first builddings on Coates street, north side, above Ridge avenue, where it remained for several years. Frederick Koline, a gentleman of large wealth, who resided part of the year in Philadelphia, on Chestnut street above Tenth street, and whose winters were spent in Charleston, South Carolina, where he owned slaves and a large property, devised by will, one hundred thousand dollars to the institution under notice. When the managers obtained this magnificent bequest, they erected their present building and sold their old site.

The building consists of two ranges, one for white, and the other for black juveniles. Seperation of these unfortunate youths of both colors and sexes is partial only, sex and color being the basis. There is a classification however, which is made of the good, worse and bad.

The House of Refuge is of brick, and embraces very many improvements in its various arrangements. It is spacious, well ventilated and warm, being heated by steam. The whole establishment wears an air of cleanliness, neatness, and comfort, quite refreshing.

THE ELECTION OF MANAGERS is by the individual contributors, who, with the present managers, are the successors of those who first established this noble charity.

PUBLIC BUILDINGS, AND COMMERCIAL BUILDINGS, AND INSTITUTIONS.

STATE HOUSE.

By direction of the Representatives of the freemen of the Province, certain lots on the south side of Chestnut street, between Fifth and Sixth streets, and extending south to Walnut street, were purchased in 1728. The cornerstone of the present State House was laid in 1729, and the building finished in 1734. In the following year it was occupied by the General Assembly of the Province, who continued its occupation until the removal of the seat of Government to Lancaster, in 1799.

The First Congress used this building during the Revolutionary War, and until 1784, when they adjourned to meet in the City of New York. The east room on the first floor, is the chamber occupied by this Congress, and in which the Independence of this Nation was declared, July 4th, 1776. This Hall is now dedicated to the public, and remains in all its fixtures, &c., as it was on that memorable event.

The two wings were added in 1790. In accordance with Acts of Assembly, one the 17th of January, 1762, and another on the 14th of May, in the same year, two lots, viz.: one on Sixth and Chestnut, and one on Fifth and Chestnut streets, were directed to be conveyed upon the payment of fifty pounds for each; the first to Trustees for the use of the County of Philadelphia, as a site for a public building for holding Courts, &c., and the second to the Mayor and Commonality of the city, for erecting a public building for city purposes. This transfer was not effected, however, until 1785. The buildings were erected in 1787-88. The City Hall was occupied from 1790 to 1800 by the Executive, Legislative, and Judicial authorities of the city and county; whilst the Congress of the United States, having removed from New York, in 1790, occupied the County Court Building, until the final transfer of the Government to Washington, in 1800.

In 1812 the Legislature authorized the County Commissioners to occupy the east and west rooms of the State House, for the accommodation of the public officers of the county. By authority of this act, those wings were enlarged, adapted, and have ever since been occupied by these officers.

In 1818 the State House, with the whole of the square &c., was transferred to the City, by the State, for the sum of $70,000, conditioned "that the square should forever remain an open walk for public use, and that *no building whatever should be erected thereon.*"

When these buildings were erected, it was thought their location was, or would be the centre of the city; while their size and accommodation were supposed ample for all the purposes of, not only the State, but of the City and County governments. Yet but few years, comparatively, have passed, and they are now found to be far from the centre of the city, and totally inadequate for the use of City Officers alone. Here then, we realize the forethought of William Penn, who, in the plan of his city, appropriated the Penn Square for the erection of a City Hall and other public buildings.

In addition to the State House, City Hall, and County Court House, the Corporation own the various Halls, (formerly occupied by the governments of the Districts previous to "Consolidation." None of them are particularly noted for historical recollections or architectural merit) and the various gas works, water works, and Alms House, previously noted.

NAVY YARD.

This national establishment is situated on Front street, below Washington avenue; entrance from the foot of Federal street. Visitors can have access to it *via* Second Street Passenger, and the Union Passenger Railway cars.

The ground embraces twelve acres, and contains all the necessary means for the construction of the largest class of war vessels. The various buildings are the officers' residences, quarters for Marines, moulding lofts, workshops, store houses, ship houses, and a sectional floating dry dock of nine sections, capable of raising the largest ship of the line.

The yard is open daily to visitors, except between the hours of 12 and 1 o'clock.

THE UNITED STATES ARSENAL, near Frankford, is a large establishment for the manufacture and storage of munitions of war. Visitors are admitted to the grounds and to the buildings, upon application to the commanding officer of the post. This Arsenal and the Navy Yard will repay a visit.

THE UNITED STATES ARSENAL, *Gray's Ferry Road*, south of the Naval Asylum, access to both of which can be had by the Spruce and Pine Street Passenger Railway cars. The Arsenal is a depot for the storage of army clothing, equipage, &c., and is open daily to visitors, from 9 to 12 o'clock, A. M., and from 2 to 7 o'clock, P. M.

UNITED STATES NAVAL ASYLUM, *Gray's Ferry Road*, below South street, was founded in 1835, as a naval school and hospital for pensioners, but is used for the latter purpose only.

The principal building is of Pennsylvania marble, and has a front of 380 feet, including a centre building of 142 feet by 175 feet deep, embellished with an imposing portico of eight Ionic columns. The wings have verandahs on each story. The grounds, containing about twenty-five acres, are tastefully laid out in plots and flower beds, which, together with the pleasant situation of the Asylum, immediately on the banks of the Schuylkill, render this a delightful retreat.

The Asylum has accommodations for 400 pensioners. Visitors are admitted by application at the gate.

UNITED STATES MINT—Chestnut street, below Broad. This structure is in the Ionic order, and presents a front on Chestnut street of over 100 feet, and extends back to Penn square.

As a specimen of street architecture it is quite an ornament. The columns and entablature are of solid marble; the rest of the structure is of brick, faced with marble ashler.

The main entrance is from Chestnut street into a hall, where gentlemanly conductors await to escort you through the establishment. Visitors admitted every day (except Saturday and Sunday) between the hours of 9 and 12 o'clock.

THE CABINET OF COINS IN THIS MINT is a magnificent collection, embracing the coins of all nations and ages.

Here are specimens of the most remote antiquity, some of them coined eight hundred years before the christian era. The student of the Bible will here see the identical counterpart of the pieces of silver for which Judas betrayed his Lord and Master; here, also, he will see the "Widow's Mite;" likewise the samples of the money which Solomon says he gathered with such care.

The Chinese and Japanese coins, are perhaps the most unique of the whole collection.

The Postal Arrangements

Of the city are very complete. They consist of a central and ten branch offices, for the receipt and delivery of letters, and nearly one thousand receiving stations for posting letters. The present CENTRAL POST OFFICE, Chestnut street, east of Fifth street, was erected and occupied in 1862.

UNITED STATES MAIL STATIONS.

Station A.—No. 41 South 18th street.
" B.—Market street west of 37th street.
" C.—S. E. corner Coates and Broad streets.
" D.—No. 1206 North 3rd street.
" E.—Richmond and William streets.
" F.—No. 90 Main street, Germantown.
" G.—Main street, below RR. Depot, Germantown.
" H.—Main street and Church avenue, Chestnut Hill.
" I.—Main street, Manayunk.
" K.—No. 502 Washington avenue.

Post Offices open daily (Sundays excepted) from 6.30, A. M., to 8 o'clock, P. M. On Sunday from 7.30 to 9.30 o'clock, A. M., and from 5 to 6 o'clock, P. M.

THE STATION BOXES for receiving letters are scattered all over the city, nearly 500 of them being attached to lamp-posts at the corner of leading streets; the rest in prominent stores and hotels.

All letters must be prepaid.

The Branch Offices may be considered as complete for all purposes of the public, as the Central Office, inasmuch as they all sell postage stamps for the pre-payment of letters. Letters for mailing, after 4 o'clock P.M., should be taken direct to the Central office. The last returns from the Branch offices close for the day at that hour.

Letters, if properly prepaid with stamps, can be dropped into any of the station boxes without trouble or inquiry, and their delivery will be as prompt as if put into any of the offices.

THE CUSTOM HOUSE,

Is situated on Chestnut street, west of Fourth.

THE BUILDING has two fronts, one on Chestnut street and one on Library street, each being ornamented by eight columns of the Doric order, 27 feet high and 4 feet 6 inches in diameter, and supporting a heavy entablature of the same order.

As viewed from Chestnut street, the edifice has a rich, chaste, and elegant appearance. It is justly regarded one of the most beautiful structures in this country.

The building was originally erected as a Banking House, at a cost of over $500,000. Subsequently, owing to the failure of the institution for which it was designed, it was purchased by the general Government, and appropriated to its present use, for which it is admirably adapted.

THE PRINCIPAL DEPARTMENT is 81 feet long, by 48 feet wide, and is richly ornamented. In addition to the Collector of Customs' office, it contains desks all neatly and conveniently arranged as follows:

No. 1, Fees; No. 2, Deputy Collector; Nos. 3, and 4, Estimating Duties; No. 5, Liquidating Duties; No. 6, Impost Bookkeeper: No. 7, Examination and Appraisements; No. 8, Bonds; No. 9, Warehousing and Withdrawals; No. 10, Re-warehousing, Transportation and exportation; Nos. 11 and 12, General Order; No. 13, Foreign Entrance and Clearance; No. 14, Registers, Enrolments and Licences; No. 15, Marine Hospital, Protections and Clearance coastwise; No. 16, Cashier, Duties and Disbursements.

Office hours from 9, A. M.. to 3 o'clock, P. M.

THE NAVAL OFFICER occupies the second story, northeast room of the Custom House. The desks of his Deputies and Clerks are as follows:

No. 1, Deputy Naval Officers; No. 2, Estimating Clerk; No. 3, Liquidating Clerk; No. 4, Clearance and Examination of Manifests; No. 5, Warehouse and Withdrawal Clerk; No. 6, Re-warehouse and Withdrawal Clerk; No. 7, Fee and Cash Clerk; No. 8, Impost Clerk; No. 9, Abstract Clerk.

THE SURVEYOR OF THE PORT.—Office in the southeast room of the Custom House, up stairs. His assistants embrace one Deputy Surveyor, a Tonnage Clerk, and a Sealing and Branding Clerk.

THE STOREKEEPER OF CUSTOMS occupies the east end room, up stairs.

APPRAISER'S OFFICE—Northeast corner of Front and Lombard streets.

INSPECTOR'S OFFICE—No. 506 South Delaware avenue.

WEIGHERS', GAUGER'S, AND MEASURER'S are also found at the Inspector's Office.

ASSISTANT TREASURER OF THE UNITED STATES—Custom House; entrance on Library street.

BANKS.

Philadelphia possesses 31 Banking Institutions, with an aggregate capital of $15,471,350. In the opinion of commercial men, this capital should be double, to meet the wants and requirements of its trade.

The Banks are open daily, Sundays and general holidays excepted, from 10 A. M., to 3 P. M.

BANK OF NORTH AMERICA.—Chestnut street, west of Third.

This was the *first* banking institution established in the United States. It, through the influence and exertions of Robert Morris, came to the aid of the Republic when all appeared dark and hopeless for want of means or credit, and loaned both to the Government. It is historical, that without this aid then given, the Department of Finance *could not* have performed its duties, the consequence of which would have been most calamitous to the cause of American Liberty.

The first charter to the Bank, was from Congress, in 1781. An additional act of incorporation was granted by the Legislature of Pennsylvania, in 1782. This was repealed in 1785, in consequence of the prejudice of country members. Mr. Morris, who knew the incalculable benefits derived by the country from the pecuniary loans of the Bank, struggled ably in its defence, and a new charter, obtained in 1787, rewarded his zeal.

The capital of the institution is $1,000,000, and the Banking House, a brown stone structure in the Italian style, is one of the most elegant buildings of the kind in its vicinity.

FARMERS' AND MECHANICS' NATIONAL BANK.—Chestnut street, west of Fourth, north side, was instituted in 1807, and chartered in 1809. The original capital was $750,000, but has subsequently been increased to $2,000,000. The Banking House of this institution, together with that of the

PHILADELPHIA NATIONAL BANK, adjoining, rank as the finest structures of the kind in the United States. The last named institution was chartered in 1804. Capital, $1,500,000.

THE NATIONAL BANK OF NORTHERN LIBERTIES—Vine street, north side, east of Third street. This institution was chartered in 1813. Its capital is $500,000.

THE MECHANICS' NATIONAL BANK—South Third street, between Market and Chestnut streets, was chartered in 1814. Capital, $800,000.

THE COMMERCIAL NATIONAL BANK—No. 314 Chestnut street; also chartered in 1814. Capital, $1,000,000.

THE NATIONAL BANK OF GERMANTOWN—Main street, Germantown. Chartered, 1814. Capital, $200,000.

GIRARD NATIONAL BANK BUILDING—Third below Chestnut street.

Demands particular notice, inasmuch as it was the first public edifice erected in this city with a portico and columns. The style and execution of its decorations, are yet unsurpassed by modern efforts.

The corner stone was laid in 1795, and the building occupied by "The Bank of the United States," in 1798. The design of the structure, is said to be a copy of the Dublin Exchange. It presents a front on Third street of 96 feet, and extends 72 feet in depth.

This building subsequently became the Banking House of Stephen Girard, and was used by him as such until his death. At present, the Girard National Bank occupies the south end of the first story as a banking room. The north end of the same floor forms the City Treasurer's office.

SOUTHWARK NATIONAL BANK, Second street below South, west side. This was the next bank instituted, having received its charter in 1825. Capital, $250,000.

MANUFACTURERS' NATIONAL BANK, north west corner of Vine and Third streets. This institution, chartered in 1832, has a capital of $570,150.

NATIONAL BANK OF COMMERCE, No. 211 Chestnut street, was chartered in 1832. Capital, $250,000.

NATIONAL BANK OF THE REPUBLIC, 809 and 811 Chestnut street. Capital $500,000.

KENSINGTON NATIONAL BANK, No. 969 Beach street, 18th Ward. Chartered in 1826. Capital, $250,000.

PENN NATIONAL BANK, located at the N. W. corner of Sixth and Vine streets, received its charter in 1828. Capital, $350,000.

WESTERN NATIONAL BANK, Chestnut street above Fourth, south side. Chartered 1832. Capital, $400,000.

TRADESMENS' NATIONAL BANK, S. W. corner of Spruce and Second streets. Chartered 1847. Capital, $200,000.

CONSOLIDATION NATIONAL BANK, No. 329 N. Third street, was incorporated in 1855. Capital, $300,000.

CITY NATIONAL BANK, No. 32 North Sixth street. Incorporated in 1855. Capital, $400,000.

COMMONWEALTH NATIONAL BANK, S. W. corner of Chestnut and Fourth streets. Incorporated in 1839. Capital, $237,000.

UNION NATIONAL BANK, N. E. corner of Third and Arch streets. Incorporated 1857. Capital, $250,000.

CORN EXCHANGE NATIONAL BANK, N. E. corner of Second and Chestnut streets. Incorporated in 1858. Capital, $500,000.

NATIONAL STATE BANK OF CAMDEN, N. J. Office No. 212 Church street, Philadelphia. Chartered in 1812. Capital, $260,000.

FIRST NATIONAL BANK AT CAMDEN, N. J. Office in this city, N. E. corner of Second and Chestnut streets. Capital, $179,000

CENTRAL NATIONAL BANK, No. 109 South Fourth street. Capital, $750,000.

FIRST NATIONAL BANK, No. 313 Chestnut street. The first National Bank established under the "national currency act;" are now erecting a banking house of the finest character. Capital, $1,000,000.

SECOND NATIONAL BANK, Main street, Frankford. Capital, $100,000.

THIRD NATIONAL BANK, No. 1424 Market street. Capital, $200,000.

NATIONAL EXCHANGE BANK, N. W. corner of Second and Green streets. Capital, $200,000.

FOURTH NATIONAL BANK, No. 723 Arch street. Capital, $150,000.

SIXTH NATIONAL BANK, No. 504 South Second street. Capital, $150,000.

SEVENTH NATIONAL BANK, No. 216 Market street. Capital, $250,000.

EIGHTH NATIONAL BANK, No. 1017 N. Second street. Capital, $275,000.

BANK CLEARING HOUSE.—No. 429 Chestnut street.

Saving Fund Societies.

PHILADELPHIA SAVING FUND SOCIETY, Seventh and Walnut streets.

WESTERN SAVING FUND, S. W. corner of Walnut and Tenth streets.

FIVE PER CENT. SAVING FUND OF THE AMERICAN TRUST COMPANY, S. E. corner of Walnut and Fourth street.

FRANKLIN SAVING FUND SOCIETY, No. 136 South Fourth street.

SAVING FUND SOCIETY OF GERMANTOWN, Main and Laurel streets, Germantown.

BENEFICIAL SAVING FUND SOCIETY OF PHILADELPHIA, S. W. corner of Twelfth and Chestnut streets.

Insurance Companies.

There are eighty-three Fire, two Marine, twelve Fire and Marine, and thirty Life; making a total of one hundred and twenty-seven Insurance Companies, in Philadelphia.

Philadelphia Board of Trade.

Rooms, No. 505 Chestnut street, second story.

The object of this Board is, to make the association a point of union among the merchants and business men of the city; where suggestions can be exchanged and discussed for the promotion of the trade and interests in Philadelphia.

The rooms of the Board are supplied with newspapers, pamphlets, public reports, books, &c. The stated annual meeting is held in February, at which valuable reports on the trade, industry, and general interest of the city are read.

Several great public movements, of not only city but national importance, have in many cases been associated with the Board of Trade. Some of them originated by its agencies.

PHILADELPHIA CORN EXCHANGE ASSOCIATION.—Hall, Second street and Exchange Alley, below Chestnut street. This association is composed of dealers in flour, grain, and other domestic produce. The Hall is open daily for sales and commercial transactions.

THE PHILADELPHIA EXCHANGE BUILDING, fronts on Dock, Third and Walnut streets.

The west entrance is on Third street, and the east or principal entrance on Dock street, both of which are embellished with elegant porticos; that on Dock street being circular, and the columns in the Corinthian order, has a fine appearance, and is much admired.

The structure is of Pennsylvania marble, and is three stories high. The first is occupied principally by Brokers and Insurance Companies; the second floor is occupied as a reading room, in which newspapers are on file from all parts of the United States, Canada, and Europe.

THE BOARD OF BROKERS, also, have their chamber in this building. In the Rotunda, what is called the "Outside Board" meet. Here public sales of stock are held, when

> Many prospects, seeming bright and fair,
> Vanish, like castles in the air.

THE COMMERCIAL ASSOCIATION have, likewise, rooms in this story. To facilitate mercantile transactions, the American, Independent, and People's Telegraph Companies, have branch offices in the rotunda.

The third story is occupied by private offices, &c. This noble building belongs to a corporate association.

BRIDGES.

THE PERMANENT BRIDGE over the Schuylkill river, at Market street. This structure was erected in 1788 by an incorporated company, but was subsequently transferred to the city, and thenceafter opened to the public as a free bridge. The whole length of the structure is 1300 feet, and rests upon three arches and two stone piers. The Market Street Passenger cars cross the bridge.

THE SUSPENSION BRIDGE at Callowhill street, Fairmount.—This light and graceful structure was built by the city. It is crossed by the Hestonville, Mantua, and Fairmount Passenger cars. The site was formerly occupied by a beautiful structure of a single elliptical arch of 348 feet span. It was destroyed by fire in 1839.

GIRARD AVENUE BRIDGE, at Girard Avenue, above Fairmount. Adjoining this is a new bridge intended for THE NEW YORK AND WASHINGTON THROUGH LINE RAILROAD.

THE COLUMBIA OR READING RAILROAD BRIDGE, is situated about half a mile above the last two. It is owned and used by the Reading Railroad, who also owns the elegant STONE BRIDGE above Laurel Hill. This last was built for the accommodation of the coal trade at Richmond, (Nineteenth Ward.)

THE PHILADELPHIA, WILMINGTON AND BALTIMORE RAILROAD BRIDGE at Gray's Ferry. In addition to its use as a railroad bridge it is also constructed to admit the passage of ordinary carriages, &c.

THE CHESTNUT STREET BRIDGE is fully acknowledged to be one of the most substantial and elegant bridges in the United States.

The Pennsylvania Central Railroad Company own the Bridge that spans the Schuylkill below South street.

CITY TOBACCO WAREHOUSE.—An immense brick structure, with stone dressings, five stories high, situated on Dock, Front, and Spruce streets. Occupied by the Warehousing Company of Philadelphia.

CITY ARMORY, Broad, below Race street.

EDUCATION.

The City of Philadelphia constitutes the first School District of the State, and is under the jurisdiction of a

BOARD OF CONTROLLERS OF PUBLIC SCHOOLS, who are elected by the Sectional School Directors, in June, annually, for a term of one year. They organize in the

ROOMS OF THE BOARD OF CONTROLLERS, Athenæum Building, Sixth and Adelphi street.

THE DISTRICT comprises twenty-six School Sections. Each under the supervision of a

BOARD OF DIRECTORS, who are elected by the people for a term of three years. It embraces one High School; one Normal School for females; fifty-eight Grammar Schools; sixty-six Secondary Schools; one hundred and eighty-one Primary Schools, and fifty unclassified schools. These schools employ eighty-two male, and one thousand one hundred and twelve female teachers, and are attended by thirty-four thousand six hundred and fifty male, and thirty-four thousand three hundred and fifty female scholars, or a total of sixty-nine thousand children.

The Central High School is admirably located on the corner of Broad and Green streets. The building is constructed of brick, in a substantial manner. Though simple in design, and built more for utility than otherwise, it presents externally both a neat and ornamental appearance.

Girls' High and Normal School—Sergeant street, between Ninth and Tenth.

This is a fine brick structure, but of much less pretensions than the Central High School.

No school in the district has so well fulfilled the expectations of its friends, so entirely accomplished the purposes of its foundation as the Normal School.

Girard College.

This magnificent Institution is pleasantly situated on Ridge avenue, north of Girard avenue. Access may be had to it *via* the Ridge Avenue Passenger cars. Visitors are admitted by tickets which can be obtained at the office of the Trustees of the Girard Estate, No. 19 South Fifth street; or at the Mayor's Office; or from R. Vaux, Esq., No. 520 Walnut street, room No. 3, first floor.

This College was founded by Stephen Girard, formerly a wealthy merchant of Philadelphia, and is designed for the support and gratuitous instruction of destitute orphans. For this purpose he devised certain funds. The City of Philadelphia is the Trustee, and the Directors of the college are its agents in the management of the institution.

The corner stone of the main edifice was laid July 4th, 1833. The buildings were completed in 1847, and the Institution opened 1848. The whole cost of the construction and fitting out of the college and adjoining buildings was about two million dollars, ($2,000,000.)

The college building is one of the most beautiful in this country, the design being that of a Grecian Temple in the Corinthian order. A colonade of eight columns on each end, and eleven on each side, surround the edifice. These columns are richly and elegantly executed. There are few cities that possess a more beautiful building than this college, or one in which chasteness of design, richness of decoration and exquisite skill of workmanship, are more happily combined.

The grounds contain about forty-one acres, the eastern portion being laid out in walks and garden plots. The entrances are, one on the north and one on the south front.

THE BOARD OF DIRECTORS OF GIRARD COLLEGE, consist of eighteen members, three of whom are elected by each chamber of councils, annually, in June. The Board organize in July, and elect the

OFFICERS OF THE INSTITUTION.—These consist of the *President of the College*, and five male and nine female teachers; one Secretary, and Superintendent of binding out; a Matron; four Perfects; five Governesses; a Farmer; two Physicians, and a Dentist. Richard Vaux, Esq., is President of the Board of Directors.

THE UNIVERSITY OF PENNSYLVANIA—Ninth street, between Chestnut and Market streets.

This Institution was first established as a simple Academy in Fourth street, below Arch, about 1744 or '45. Subsequently it was enlarged into a College, and finally into its present extended field of operations. The Medical Department of the University, was the first Medical College in the United States.

This Institution is under the direction of a Board of twenty-five trustees. The Governor of the State of Pennsylvania being ex-officio President of the Board.

The University is divided into Departments, viz.: *The Department of Arts, of Medicine, of Law, of Mines, Arts, and Manufactures, and of the Fine Arts.*

MEDICAL SCHOOLS, &c.

THE MEDICAL DEPARTMENT of the University is under the immediate government of the Medical Professors, who constitute the Faculty.

As a means of illustrating and forcibly impressing the lessons of the lecture room

CLINICAL instruction in Medicine and Surgery is conducted in the University Hall, four times a week, throughout the session.

The College contains one of the richest medical museums in the country.

JEFFERSON MEDICAL COLLEGE—Tenth street, above Walnut, bears a high reputation as a medical school, and has also extensive hospital accommodations, which forms part of the clinic of the Institution.

THE PHILADELPHIA UNIVERSITY OF MEDICINE AND SURGERY—Ninth street, below Locust. This institution possesses every convenience for a full and thorough course of medical instruction.

* ECLECTIC MEDICAL COLLEGE OF PENNSYLVANIA—N. E. corner of Sixth and Callowhill streets.

MEDICAL SOCIETY OF THE STATE OF PENNSYLVANIA—No. 215 Spruce street.

AMERICAN MEDICAL ASSOCIATION—No. 215 Spruce street.

COLLEGE OF PHYSICIANS OF PHILADELPHIA—Instituted 1787, and incorporated 1789—N. E. corner of Thirteenth and Locust streets. This College holds monthly meetings to discuss medical subjects, &c. These proceedings are published in a quarterly report, a work justly regarded as one of the most valuable medical periodicals of the day.

NORTHERN MEDICAL ASSOCIATION OF THE STATE OF PENNSYLVANIA—No. 603 Spring Garden street. This association meets twice a month.

HOMEOPATHIC MEDICAL COLLEGE OF PENNSYLVANIA—Filbert, below Twelfth street.

THE FEMALE MEDICAL COLLEGE OF PENNSYLVANIA—Founded in 1849, was the first of the kind ever established for the medical education of women. The institution is pleasantly located on North College avenue and Twenty-second street.

THE PENNSYLVANIA COLLEGE OF DENTAL SURGERY—S. E. corner of Tenth and Arch streets.

THE PHILADELPHIA DENTAL COLLEGE—No. 108 North Tenth street.

THE PHILADELPHIA COLLEGE OF PHARMACY—Filbert street, above Seventh, is the oldest institution of the kind in the United States.

ALUMNI ASSOCIATION—No. 816 Filbert street.

PHILADELPHIA COUNTY MEDICAL SOCIETY—Instituted in 1807.

THEOLOGICAL SCHOOLS, &c.

Comprise THE THEOLOGICAL SEMINARY OF THE REFORMED PRESBYTERIAN CHURCH, Broad street, below Spruce; PHILADELPHIA DIVINITY SCHOOL, Thirty-ninth and Walnut streets—Office, No. 708 Walnut street; ST. JOSEPH'S COLLEGE, Filbert and Juniper streets; SEMINARY OF ST. CHARLES BORROMEO, N. E.

corner of Eighteenth and Race streets, (*Theological*), supported by the annual voluntary contributions of the Catholics of the Diocese.

ACADEMY OF THE PROTESTANT EPISCOPAL CHURCH—Locust street, near Broad.

ST. MARK'S EPISCOPAL ACADEMY—Locust street, west of Sixteenth.

UNIVERSITY OF PENNSYLVANIA.

Educational Associations.

Hebrew Education Society—Seventh street, below Callowhill. Hebrew is taught in this school according to both the Portuguese and German customs. This is one of the best Hebrew schools in the country, where that language is taught in its purity.

The Polytechnic College of the State of Pennsylvania—Market street and West Penn Square. This is a private institution, organized on the plan of the Industrial Colleges of France and Germany.

The Philadelphia Institute for Colored Youths—Shippen street, near Ninth. The instruction in this Academy embraces, in addition to the ordinary branches of a good English education, mathematics, natural sciences, and the classics.

Association of Friends, for the free instruction of adult colored persons. Office, No. 817 Arch street.

The Board of Education of the Presbyterian Church, occupy the fine building on Chestnut street opposite the United States Mint.

The Pennsylvania Baptist Educational Society—No. 530 Arch street.

THE PHILADELPHIA TRAINING SCHOOL FOR FEEBLE MINDED CHILDREN—Office, No. 530 Walnut street.

This is one of the many noble institutions that mark the present age of an enlightened community, and whose establishment reflects more real glory on their founders and patrons, than ever bestowed upon a whole army of Alexanders and Napoleons. It is located at Media, Delaware county, where elegant and well adapted buildings, with ample grounds, accommodate over one hundred and fifty pupils.

PENNSYLVANIA INSTITUTION FOR THE INSTRUCTION OF THE BLIND.

This noble charity is situated at the corner of Race and Twentieth streets, and is convenient of access by the Race and Vine, and Arch Streets Passenger Railways. It can also be reached by the 17th and 19th Streets Passenger Railway.

The Institution is open to visitors every Wednesday at 2½ o'clock P.M., when an opportunity is afforded to examine the work shops. At 3½ o'clock an Exhibition is given, consisting of vocal and instrumental music, and exercises with the school apparatus. A small admission fee is charged at the door. The fund derived from this source is appropriated in outfits to graduates on leaving the Institution. These exhibitions are popular with our citizens, and are largely attended.

The pupils are always occupied, except in the regular recess. Eight hours daily are devoted to school studies, music and work. Four evenings a week to reading or a lecture.

The Musical Department has a well-deserved reputation. The orchestra consists of thirty-two instruments. The public performances on Wednesday afternoons, comprise some of the finest overtures and other compositions of eminent masters. The musical department also contains a chorus of forty voices.

The Manufacturing Department is perhaps the most interesting part of the establishment. Here the pupils are instructed in useful trades, which give employment to many worthy blind persons.

A Home of Industry for the Blind of this School, who have no friends to receive them, is established as a branch of the Institution. In this retreat they can earn their support, while their morals will be protected, and a just estimate put on their talents, and their earnings will be secured to them. The attention of the benevolent is called to this part of the Institution. By their aid, its usefulness can be largely extended.

The Pennsylvania Institution for the Deaf and Dumb,

located on the N. W. corner of Broad and Pine streets, was incorporated in 1821, when the Legislature endowed it with a grant of eight thousand dollars, and also provided for the payment of a stipulated sum per annum, for the support and education of every indigent child of suitable age in the State of Pennsylvania, which should be admitted to the institution, provided the annual payment should not exceed eight thousand dollars.

The States of Maryland, New Jersey, and Delaware, have also made provision for the education of deaf mutes, native of their respective states, in this Institution.

By the rules of the Institution, deaf and dumb children are not admitted under ten years of age.

No stranger should leave the city without paying a visit to the two last named institutions.

THE BLIND ASYLUM.

LITERARY AND SCIENTIFIC ASSOCIATIONS.

The American Philosophical Society—situated on Fifth street, below Chestnut, sprang from the famous "Junto," a club organized in 1727, and composed of a limited number of ardent and enterprising young men, of whom Benjamin Franklin was the leading and active spirit.

This club appears to have been a conversational society, at whose meetings, public events, measures and projects for the improvement of themselves or the city, were freely debated. They seem to have been very active and successful in establishing various social reforms, prominent among which were several associations for the promotion of useful knowledge.

In May, 1743, the "Junto" issued a prospectus for "the formation of a society for the promotion of useful knowledge among the British Provinces of North America." This prospectus was signed by Benjamin Franklin as Secretary. In 1744, nine gentlemen having responded to the project, the society was formed. Of these original nine, six were members of the "Junto." The first Officers elected were, Thomas Hopkinson, President, ——— Coleman, Treasurer, and Benjamin Franklin, Secretary.

For several years this society appears to have existed but in name, for we find that in November, 1767, but five or six of the members remained. These made an effort, and succeeded in reviving the society; over forty new members were added, and on the 9th day of February, 1768, Ex-Governor Hamilton was elected President. In 1769, a similar association, that appears to have existed as a rival, was merged into the one under notice, and thus formed the present AMERICAN PHILOSOPHICAL SOCIETY for the promotion of useful knowledge. The first officers of the consolidated society were Benjamin Franklin, President, and Dr. Thomas Cadwallader, Dr. Thomas Bond, and Joseph Galloway, Esq., Vice Presidents. The society was incorporated March 15th, 1780.

The site of their present Hall was granted to them by Act of Assembly in 1785, and the building erected and occupied in 1790. The society occupies the second story, the first story and basement being rented to the city, for the accommodation of public offices.

The Library is a fine room, neatly fitted up with cases, &c. It contains about 25,000 volumes of the most valuable description. Some of the works in this Library cannot be duplicated in America. It is rich, also, in manuscripts, letters and papers of the rarest kind, and whose intrinsic value cannot be over-estimated.

The Cabinet is a fine one; the room, however, is entirely too small for the collection.

The Committee-room is a cozy chamber, remarkable as being the scene of many a festive meeting between the illustrious of by-gone days. Here, Washington, Franklin, Jefferson, Rittenhouse, Wistar, Hamilton, Adams, Tilghman, Duponceau, Lafayette, and a host of like spirits, met to enjoy "the feast of reason and flow of soul," untrammelled by the cares of state.

HISTORICAL SOCIETY OF PENNSYLVANIA— Athenæum Building, Sixth and Adelphi streets, having for its object, the elucidation of the history of this State, was instituted December 2d, 1824.

The Society's museum possesses a number of valuable relics, many of which have been received from the Governments of the United

States, of Pennsylvania, of Great Britain, as well as from foreign and American societies, and from the family of William Penn.

The rooms are open every Monday, from 8 A.M. to 10 o'clock P.M., except during July and August.

THE ACADEMY OF NATURAL SCIENCES—is situated on the N. W. corner of Broad and Sansom streets. This institution was founded in 1812, and incorporated in 1817. Tickets of admission can be obtained from Mr. E. Parrish, 800 Arch street.

The academy building is of brick, constructed fire proof. It is void of display in exterior design and finish. The structure presents two stories resting upon a rusticated basement. The windows on the east and west ends occupy nearly the entire front. The entrance on Broad street is used by visitors to the museum; that on Sansom street by the members, &c.

THE LIBRARY contains over 23,000 volumes, exclusive of maps, periodicals, serials and pamphlets, of which it has an immense number. The books are neatly arranged according to subjects. It is rich in works on Natural Science, Anatomy, and Physiology, the transactions of Societies, Journals, Memoirs, &c., and Historical Documents of all descriptions. It also contains some valuable works on Antiquities and the Fine Arts.

THE COLLECTION OF REPTILES, is placed in the galleries of the east and north-east rooms. This collection, it is believed, is not surpassed by many in Europe.

THE PRINCIPAL ROOM OF THE ACADEMY, occupies the

entire upper story. It is one hundred and ten feet long, and forty feet wide, and is lighted from the roof, and from the east and west ends. Ranges of graceful galleries run along the sides and ends. These galleries, with the exception of the lowest or flying gallery, are supported by light iron columns, and are fitted up with cases. The floor is occupied by ranges of horizontal cases, running the whole depth of the hall, and each of these ranges are surmounted on its centre line by a series of vertical cases, glazed on both sides.

THE COLLECTION OF MAMMALOGY placed in cases on the floor of this main saloon, beneath the north gallery, though not extensive, possesses considerable interest.

THE BIRDS, placed in cases along the galleries, is one of the largest and most valuable collections in the world; they form the chief attraction of the room, rendering brilliancy to every part of it. In connection with these birds, there is a fine collection of nests and eggs, which will be found in shallow cases, suspended from the railing of the lowest gallery. This collection of eggs is also unequalled by any other, even in Europe.

THE COLLECTION OF INSECTS is arranged in boxes made to resemble folio volumes.

THE COLLECTION OF PLANTS, &c., is to be found in cases on the north flying gallery. This herbarium is allowed by all judges, to be one of the richest and most valuable in the world.

On the south flying gallery, the visitor will find DR. MORTON'S CELEBRATED COLLECTION OF CRANIA. In a closet opening on the passage to the stairs, at the south-east extremity of this gallery, are four human mummies, Egyptian and Peruvian, together with several mummied Egyptian "gods." The Egyptian subjects are of great antiquity.

The various magnificent collections in this Academy, would require a volume to do justice to their merits. We cannot even enumerate them.

THE PENNSYLVANIA HORTICULTURAL SOCIETY. Broad below Locust street. Instituted, 1827. Incorporated, 1831. Is the oldest Horticultural Society in the United States. Its large and valuable library, the most extensive of its kind in this country, has been the means of disseminating a vast deal, not only of horticultural knowledge, but of information on other kindred topics of natural science.

The Hall is stately and commodious, centrally situated, and well adapted for the purposes of the Society. It is open every Tuesday evening.

ATHENÆUM—Sixth and Adelphia streets, is another noble institution, owing its origin to that taste for literary pursuits which has always characterized this city.

In the year 1813, six young men feeling the want of a convenient place of common resort, in which their leisure hours could be passed agreeably and pleasantly, arranged a plan for a reading room. Which of these young men was the first or prime mover in this enterprise, we are not informed. The six, however, seem to have acted with energy, for we find that by the 9th of February, 1814, they had obtained two hundred subscribers. On that day, articles of association were adopted, and the first Board of officers and Directors elected. In a few weeks thereafter the Institution was opened to the public, in rooms over "Carey's Book Store," South-east corner of Chestnut and Fourth streets.

The corner-stone of the present building was laid November 1, 1845, and the Hall opened in 1847.

This building is a chaste and elegant structure of two

stories, resting on a rusticated basement. It presents a front of fifty feet on Sixth street, and one hundred and twenty-five feet on Adelphia street.

The design of the building is the "Italian," of which style of architecture it is an excellent specimen, treated with spirit and taste. The basement story is of a rich brown stone, and rests on moulded plinth. A moulded band and frieze marks the division of this and the main story.

The first story is divided into offices, most of which are occupied by the Controllers of Public Schools.

A spacious stairway of easy ascent, leads to the principal story. This is arranged for the uses of the Athenæum, and is divided into a Library, News Room, and a Chess Room.

The News Room fronts on Sixth street. It is 37 by 47 feet, and 24 feet high; it is neatly finished in pilasters, with an enriched cornice. The Chess Room is an ante room between the News Room and Library.

The Historical Society of Pennsylvania, occupy the front room of the third story of the Athenæum Building. It contains about 23,000 volumes, well selected, and is richly supplied with the periodicals and newspapers of both this and foreign countries.

The entire cost of the Athenæum Building, including fitting up, was about $50,000.

THE FRANKLIN INSTITUTE—Seventh street, above Chestnut, was incorporated in 1824, for the promotion and encouragement of manufacture and the mechanic arts. The Hall is a plain building, and contains a Lecture Room, a Library, and Cabinet of Minerals, and a few models.

THE PENNSYLVANIA AGRICULTURAL SOCIETY—Open every Wednesday at 12 M. Office, No. 702 Walnut street.

PHILADELPHIA LYCEUM—S. E. corner of Ninth and Spring Garden streets. THE PHILADELPHIA CITY INSTITUTE—N. E. corner of Eighteenth and Chestnut streets. THE SPRING GARDEN INSTITUTE—Spring Garden and Broad streets. THE KENSINGTON INSTITUTE—Richmond and Shackamaxon streets. THE MOYAMENSING INSTITUTE—S. E. corner of Eleventh and Catharine streets. THE WEST PHILADELPHIA INSTITUTE—Thirty-ninth and Market streets. THE WAGNER FREE INSTITUTE OF SCIENCE—Seventeenth street and Montgomery avenue, are flourishing Institutions, possessing valuable libraries. Their Halls, most of which are of recent construction, are well supplied with newspapers and periodicals. Lectures are also given in them during the season; these lectures are very popular, and are well attended.

To enumerate all the various Literary Associations, which abound in and ornament our city, would far exceed our limits.

FINE ARTS.

PENNSYLVANIA ACADEMY OF FINE ARTS, No. 1028 Chestnut street. This Institution was founded in 1805, and incorporated in 1806. The Academy is a joint stock association. An annual exhibition is held in the spring, for a period of six weeks. Other exhibitions are held during the year. To these, American Artists are invited to send their productions. Works of distinguished merit from private collections, are then also displayed.

The walls of the picture gallery are now covered with paintings of the ancient and modern schools, many of them by masters of the highest celebrity. Among them we notice "Death on the Pale Horse," "Paul and Barnabus," "The Prodigal Son's Return," "The Triumph of Love," "Scene from the Tempest," and "The Battle of Bender," all by Sir Benjamin West; "The Dead Man restored to Life, by touching the Bones of the Prophet Elisha," by Washington Allston; "The March of Silenus," by Rubens; "The Deliverance of Leyden," by Wittkamp, together with several fine pictures from the pencils of Sully, Stewart, Winner, Rothermel, Valasquer, Inman, Van Gayer, Salvator Rosa, David, Peale, Zucatelli, Schedoni, Neagle &c.

Among the many interesting objects of sculpture, are several by Thorwaldsen, Canova, Ceracchi, Stienhauer, Greenough, Lough, Thom, &c.

THE LIBRARY is adorned with many splendid works of

engraving in all its various departments, as well as with some valuable volumes on its art.

The Academy is open daily for visitors, and is one of the most attractive places of resort in Philadelphia.

PHOTOGRAPHERS abound in all quarters of the city.

ENGRAVERS.—This branch of the fine arts is divided into Bank Note Engravers, Copper and Steel; Engravers and Die-sinkers; Historical, Portrait, and Landscape; Map; Card; Calico Printers; Wood, &c. The number employed in each of these branches, cannot now be ascertained, but some idea may be formed when we state that there are over fifty establishments in the city, some of whom employ twenty artists, none less than two.

CHARLES F. HASELTINE'S GALLERIES—1125 Chestnut street.—These are the most important Galleries in the country for the Free Exhibition of works of art of a high character. In these Galleries at any season of the year may be seen paintings by the best French, English, German, Italian, Flemish, and American Painters. The collection is continually changing, for the pictures being for sale, and being sold, causes a constant addition of new works to take the place of those disposed of. The Galleries are on the second floor. The first floor is devoted to the sale of Engravings, Chromos, Looking Glasses, and Artists' Materials. We notice amongst the old engravings, specimens of Morghen, Toschi, Longhi, Mercuri, Calamatta, &c., in this department. Mr Haseltine has probably the finest collection in the country for sale. The establishment itself, on account of its finish and beauty of ornamentation, forms an attractive place of high order.

LIBRARIES.

THE LIBRARY COMPANY OF PHILADELPHIA—Fifth, below Chestnut street. This Association was organized on the 8th of November, 1731. The first invoice of books was received in October, 1732. In addition to the purchased books, Mr. Collinson added two works, viz.:—"Sir Isaac Newton's Philosophy," and William Miller's "Gardener's Dictionary." His claim as first of the many subsequent donators, is thus fully established.

In glancing at this early effort, we must recollect that there was no provision by the Government, for education, nor was there a bookseller in the country, with the exception of one in Boston, and his operations were on a very small scale. We may, therefore, realize the sensation created in Philadelphia, by the arrival of this "lot of books." They were taken in great state to the house of Robert Grace, in Jones' Alley, where the first library was established. The chronicle states that the company were soon engaged in arranging and cataloguing the books. The first Librarian was Louis Timothee, who attended at the library room on Wednesdays and Saturdays.

In 1738, the collection became too large for the humble room in Jones' Alley. In 1739, the Assembly granted the company the free use of a room in the State House, to which the Library was removed in 1740. In 1769, the Union Library was united with the one under notice. In 1771, two others likewise became annexed. The value of these accessions, we have no means of ascertaining. The Union Company, appears, however, to have been of some considerable importance, inasmuch as it owned its own library building on Third street. The enterprise was now firmly established, and the collection rapidly increased, so that the room in the State House was soon found too small for its accommodation. Larger and more commodious apartments were obtained in Carpenters' Hall, to which the Library was removed in 1773, where it was opened for the first time daily. The Continental Congress enjoyed its free use during the memorable sessions of 1774, and 1775, and no doubt, its treasures were exceedingly valuable to those inquiring and patriotic minds.

In 1789 the corner stone of the present building was laid under the south-west corner of the structure. This building was finished, and the books removed, arranged, and ready for delivery on the 30th day of December, 1790.

The edifice is of brick, constructed in the most substantial manner. Though simple in design, and built more for utility than display, it presents an ornamental appearance. A fine statue of Dr. Franklin stands in a niche over the front entrance. The likeness is said to be a good one. It was executed in Italy, by the order, and at the expense of William Bingham.

Among the many valuable bequests to this institution, we notice that by the Rev. Samuel Preston, of London, to appreciate which, the collection must be examined in detail. It embraces many rare books of plates of the most costly description. The Loganian Library is also a valuable acquisition. This collection was the private library of the Hon. James Logan, the friend and counsellor of William Penn. When first annexed to the Philadelphia Library, it contained about 4000 volumes. Additions are made to it annually from a fund bequeathed by Mr. Logan for this purpose. Choice and rare books were also donated to the company by William Mackenzie and Robert Barclay, of London, and William Logan.

Among the rare books in the library, we notice several of the date of 1470, a copy of rare old Caxton's "Golden Legend," printed at Westminster, and which Caxton tells us, is *printed* not "wroten with penne and inke as other bokes ben."

In the department relating to America, the library is exceedingly rich. It contains, for instance, complete sets of newspapers, from the first number of the first paper published in Philadelphia.

Of the many manuscripts in the library, the most ancient, is a copy of the entire Bible on parchment of the 15th century, while the most beautiful is an illuminated Psalter on fine vellum, still in perfect preservation. Not the least interesting portion of the Library, is that consisting of works from the nations of Continental Europe, embracing most of the standard authors. The collection of Spanish books is the most complete, and, perhaps, the finest in the United States, except one. The Library contains at present about 85,000 volumes, and is opened daily.

THE MERCANTILE LIBRARY—Tenth above Chestnut street. This popular institution was opened in temporary rooms on Chestnut street, in 1821. Its charter bears date July 1st, 1842. The library building was erected in 1869, at a cost of over $227,000. The library is also fitted up as a reading room. It contains about 50,000 volumes, and is regularly supplied with over three hundred magazines and newspapers from every State in the Union, including Canada, with the leading journals of Great Britain, France, and Germany.

LIBRARY OF THE FRANKLIN INSTITUTE—

Seventh above Chestnut street, is composed principally of mechanical and scientific works. The reading room is well supplied with periodicals, newspapers, &c.

THE GERMAN LIBRARY—Seventh above Chestnut street. The *first* story of the building is occupied by the Trustees of the City Gas Works. This institution has about 12,000 books, principally in foreign languages. Open Wednesdays and Saturdays, from 3 to 5 o'clock, P. M.

LIBRARY OF THE PENNSYLVANIA HOSPITAL—Occupies an elegant room in the Hospital Building, Pine street, between Eighth and Ninth. This library contains about 13,000 volumes, mostly medical, and those pertaining to kindred sciences. As a Medical Library, it is, perhaps, the most extensive and complete in the United States.

APPRENTICES' LIBRARY, is situated in the venerable building, known as a Friend's Meeting House, at the corner of Arch and Fifth streets. This Institution was founded in 1819, for the benefit of youth, male and female. The works are selected with care, and embrace over 22,000 volumes. The library is open for boys on Monday, Wednesday, Friday, and Saturday evenings, and on Saturday afternoons, and on every afternoon, except Monday, for girls.

FRIENDS' FREE LIBRARY—No. 304 Arch

street, has about 6,500 volumes. Books are loaned to any person, irrespective of creed, nation, or color, provided the applicant produces a good moral character, vouched for by some one of the Society of Friends. Open on Thursdays from 4 to 6 o'clock, P. M., and on Saturdays from 3 to 7 o'clock, P. M.

LAW LIBRARY—County County Court House, Sixth and Chestnut streets, is composed of law-books entirely. It has about 7,500 volumes.

LIBRARY ASSOCIATION OF THE TWENTY-THIRD WARD—Wright's Institute, Frankford.

PRESBYTERIAN HISTORICAL SOCIETY, No. 821 Chestnut street.

SOUTHWARK LIBRARY, No. 765 South Second street.

GIRARD LIBRARY—S. W. corner of Sixth street and Girard avenue. JAMES PAGE FREE LIBRARY—Girard avenue, east of Shackamaxon street.

THE LIBRARY ASSOCIATION OF FRIENDS—Meeting House, Race above Fifteenth street, has about 7000 well selected works.

In addition to these there are valuable libraries attached to all the *Medical Colleges*, to the *Academy of Natural Sciences; Academy of Fine Arts; The Horticultural Society*, and to the *Pennsylvania Historical Society*, a visit to any of which will well repay the student or lover of rare and valuable works. Nor should we forget the numerous libraries attached to the various churches and religious denominations, some of great value and extent; also the libraries belonging to Literary Institutions and associations.

ST. STEPHEN'S CHURCH, (Episcopal.) Tenth Street above Chestnut.

CHURCHES IN PHILADELPHIA.

The first church erected in Philadelphia or its vicinity was at Tinicum, a small island on the Delaware, near the Lazaretto. It was founded by a colony of Swedes in 1646.

This colony and church was destroyed by the Dutch West India Company, in 1655. Several settlements, however, had been made further up the Delaware and Schuylkill, whose numbers were subsequently increased by emigration. Among these early settlements were those at Weccaco, Moyamensing, and Passyunk. For their accommodation and protection, a place of worship and a temporary fort was erected in 1677, near the site of the present Swedes Church, in Swanson street. The primitive structure was removed in 1700, when the present edifice was built. For many years this was the only place of worship on either side of the Delaware or Schuylkill.

FRIENDS' MEETING HOUSES.—The first meeting of the Society of Friends, in Philadelphia, were held at the house of Thomas Fairlamb, at Shackamaxon, near the "Treaty Ground." This was in 1681, the year Markham and the first English colonists arrived. From this it would appear that there was a previous settlement of Europeans at that place. In 1682 a frame building was erected at Centre or Penn Square, intended for the double purpose of a Meeting House for worship, and a City Hall, though it appears not to have been used for the latter purpose. In 1685 a Meeting House was erected in Front street, north of Arch. This, when the Meeting House in Pine street was built, they called the "North Meeting House," and the Pine street one, the "South Meeting House." In 1789, the North Meeting House was removed to a new building then erected in Key's alley.

In 1698, a Meeting House was erected at the southwest corner of Market and Second streets, which, after being rebuilt in 1755, was entirely removed in 1808.

There are 13 Meeting Houses in Philadelphia.

FRIENDS' MEETING HOUSE—Fourth and Arch streets. The burial ground attached to this house is the oldest, with the exception of that belonging to the Swedes' Church, in the city.

FRIENDS' MEETING HOUSE—Fifth and Arch streets. This building is now occupied by the "Apprentices' Library." It was erected by the Free Friends, or as they were called during the Revolution, "The Fighting Quakers," inasmuch as they differed from the others, in thinking it lawful to take up arms in defence of American liberty, which many of them did. We find by a sketch in the Historical Society's collection, that the last of these patriots long worshipped in this house, alone. He came regularly every first day, and spent the hours in the usual devotions.

EPISCOPALIAN CHURCHES.

From records, it appears that this denomination had a place of worship on the site of the present CHRIST CHURCH, Second above Market street, as early at 1698. The first house was a log building, rude enough in its construction. Here divine service was occasionally performed under the ministration of the Rev. Mr. Clayton until 1700, when the first regularly appointed minister was sent over by the Bishop of London. By the labors of this gentlemen, (the Rev. Evan Evans), the first congregation was regularly formed. The primitive building was subsequently enlarged and improved until 1727, when the present edifice was commenced, the west end of which was erected in that year. The east end and main body of the building was commenced in 1731, and in a few years thereafter substantially completed, with the exception of the spire as it now appears. The spire was erected in 1753. It is a graceful work of art, and contains a chime of eight bells.

CHRIST CHURCH was erected from designs by Dr. J. J. Kearsley, and built by Robert Smith. The style, decorations and construction of both church and spire, are alike creditable to their taste and skill. Few, if any, similar edifices in the city yet surpass it.

ST. PETER'S CHURCH—Third and Pine streets, was the second organized in the city. The Church building was erected in 1761. The spacious burial ground attached to this edifice adds much to its appearance. Some of the most distinguished of the early citizens of Philadelphia, are buried here. This spire also contains a fine chime of bells.

Most of the Episcopal churches are highly ornamental in their construction, particularly those of modern date. Among these we notice

ST. STEPHEN'S CHURCH—Tenth street, below Market, the facade of which presents a bold and impressive appearance. A small recessed room, adjoining the church on the north side, contains a beautiful monument dedicated to the "Burd family," long members, and liberal endowers of the church and its institutions. This building is a specimen of the Gothic architecture of the middle ages.

St. Andrew's Church—8th street, above Spruce, is a beautiful building, the front being a perfect example of the Ionic order, taken from the Temple of Bacchus at Teos. The interior of the building is highly finished.

St. Mark's Church—Locust street, above 16th. This structure is of that order of Gothic known as the " decorated," of which it is a fine specimen. The interior is much admired.

St. Jude's Church—Franklin street, above Brown; St. Matthew's Church, 18th street and Girard avenue; Church of St. James the Less, Falls of Schuylkill; Church of the Holy Trinity, 19th and Walnut streets; of the Epiphany, 15th and Chestnut streets, and of the Covenant, Filbert street, above 17th; Grace, 13th and Cherry streets; St. Clement's, 20th and Cherry streets, and St. Luke's, 13th below Spruce, are each worth the attention of the admirer of architecture.

There are 63 Episcopal churches in this city, of which one is colored.

Baptist Churches.

The Baptist denomination established a church in Philadelphia in 1698. This early effort was commenced by nine persons, who were subsequently aided by the Rev. John Watts. For awhile they appear to have met in connection with the Presbyterians, in the house, corner of

Chestnut and Second streets. In 1762 they erected the large building which yet stands, although not occupied, in La Grange Place, 2d below Arch street, and worshipped in the same, until within the last few years. The congregation composing the church having mostly removed to distant parts of the city, erected the present handsome building on the corner of Arch and Broad streets, that location being deemed more suitable for the interests of their cause.

For many years the Baptists performed the rites of immersion in the Schuylkill river, near the foot of Spruce street, a spot long celebrated for its rural beauties. Now, most if not all of these churches have baptismal pools in their buildings.

Of the most prominent buildings erected by this society, that of the FIFTH BAPTIST CHURCH, deserves particular attention as a fine example of church architecture. The FIRST BAPTIST CHURCH, Broad and Arch streets, is likewise a rich and attractive edifice.

There are 37 Baptist churches in the city, of which 4 are colored.

PRESBYTERIAN CHURCHES.

THE FIRST PRESBYTERIAN CHURCH—was established in 1698, by the Rev. Jedediah Andrews. Their primary meetings were held on the N. W. corner of Second and Chestnut streets.

In 1704 the congregation erected their first building, on Market street, between Second and Third. This they enlarged in 1729, and entirely rebuilt in 1793, on a larger and more imposing scale, so much so that it was called " The Cathedral." The building was 88 feet long, 56 wide, and 46 high. Its facade consisted of a prostyle of four Corinthian columns, which with the cornice and pediment, was highly enriched. The rapid extension of trade, caused the final removal of this edifice in 1822; the congregation having procured the much more desirable location at the corner of Locust and Seventh streets, upon which they erected their present elegant building, in 1821.

THE SECOND PRESBYTERIAN CHURCH—owes its origin to a division in the First church, caused by the preaching of the eloquent Whitfield, in 1742. These withdrew to the "Whitfield, new Meeting House," in Fourth street below Arch, subsequently known as the "Old Academy." In 1750, they founded the Second Presbyterian Church, on the corner of Arch and Third streets, which, in 1809, they rebuilt on an enlarged and more attractive scale. Owing to the noise and turmoil of its commercial neighborhood, the congregation subsequently sold the property.

THE THIRD PRESBYTERIAN CHURCH—4th and Pine streets, was founded by a colony from the church in Market street, in 1766. This ancient church was formerly under the pastoral charge of Dr. A. Alexander. Its spacious graveyard contains the remains of many famed in the annals of both church and state.

The Presbyterian church has been eminently successful, and has exerted a marked influence in the cause of humanity and religion. Ever active in the cause of benevolence, they are foremost in the origin of every charitable institution of a general character in the city.

Among the church edifices belonging to this society, worthy of note for their architectural display, is THE NORTH BROAD STREET CHURCH, situated on the corner of Broad and Green streets, of which locality it forms a prominent and attractive feature. The building is 117 feet in length on Green street, and 75 feet wide on Broad street. The tower on the west end is 25 feet broad at the base. The entire height of the tower and spire is 215 feet. The structure is of rubble stone with dressed trimmings, both of a fine quality. A large rosette window, filled with beautiful stained glass, together with the chaste decorations peculiar to this order, gives a pleasing effect to the facade on Broad street. The style of the building is the "Norman," and its cost was about $33,000.

THE FIFTH CHURCH—Arch street, above Tenth, erected in 1823, is also a beautiful structure. It is of brick, with marble dressings. The tower and spire is highly ornamental, exhibiting at one view in their proper grades, the Ionic, Corinthian and Composite orders of architecture. Refined taste questions the propriety of such a combination, yet it is not disputed that the effect is fine.

THE CALVARY CHURCH—15th and Locust streets, is likewise an elegant building. Its northern front, the only one presented to view, is highly decorated.

THE WEST ARCH STREET CHURCH—is also justly esteemed among the ornaments of the city. The rich decorations, together with its location, 18th and Arch streets, give it a grand appearance.

THE CENTRAL CHURCH, 8th and Cherry streets; THE SPRING GARDEN CHURCH, 11th above Spring Garden streets; together with the one at PENN SQUARE, that in WEST PHILADELPHIA, and the WEST SPRUCE STREET, 17th and Spruce streets, are all creditable alike to their congregations and the city.

There are 81 Presbyterian churches in the city, of which 37 are Old School, 23 New School, 10 United, 8 Reformed, and 3 colored.

There are but four DUTCH REFORMED CHURCHES in Philadelphia. THE FIRST CHURCH, an elegant building, with a lofty portico in the Corinthian order, is situated at the corner of Seventh and Spring Garden streets. THE SECOND CHURCH is located in Seventh street, above Brown. THE THIRD at the corner of Tenth and Filbert streets, and THE FOURTH at Manayunk.

THE MORAVIANS OR UNITED BRETHERN— have a church at Franklin and Wood streets, while THE NEW JERUSALEM CHURCH sustains five places of worship in the city, viz.:—*The First*, corner of Broad and Brandywine streets: *Second*, 4th street below German; *Third*, Cherry street between 21st and 22d; the *Fourth* and *Fifth* are both at Frankford.

THE LUTHERANS have 17 churches in Philadelphia, the oldest and most noted of which is at the corner of Fifth streets and Appletree alley. It was erected in 1743, and ZION'S CHURCH, Fourth street above Arch, erected 1766. Both buildings are creditable specimens of ancient style of building.

ST. JOHN'S CHURCH—Race street, above Fifth, is an elegant building.

There are 8 GERMAN REFORMED churches, of which the FIRST CHURCH, Race street below Fourth, established in 1762 is the oldest, and

CHRIST CHURCH, Green street, above Fifteenth, the most elegant and modern. The spire of Christ Church is an object of attraction in the neighborhood.

ROMAN CATHOLIC CHURCHES.

But few of the denomination appeared to have resided in the city previous to 1733. In that year the Rev. Mr. Crayton was formally commissioned by the Bishop of Maryland, to take charge of the Church in Philadelphia. This gentleman, to further his purpose, purchased a lot on Fourth Street, south of Walnut, upon which he erected a small chapel. This was dedicated to *St. Joseph*. This house was afterwards enlarged, as the wants of the community required.

In 1763, ST. MARY'S CHURCH, Fourth, below Walnut street, was erected. This building was also enlarged in 1810 to its present size. The grounds attached to the church, contain the remains of many noted citizens of this denomination. THE CHURCH OF THE HOLY TRINITY—Sixth and Spruce streets, was erected in 1789, for the accommodation of the German population; and ST. AUGUSTINE'S CHURCH—Fourth, between Race and Vine, in 1800. This latter building was destroyed by a disgraceful mob some years since, when the present neat edifice was erected.

The Diocese of Philadelphia was established in 1809. It comprises all that part of Pennsylvania east of the western limit of Tioga, Centre, Mifflin, Juniati, Franklin and Fulton counties, and also the State of Delaware. The churches in this city, belonging to the denomination, number 35, of which,

THE CATHEDRAL OF ST. PETER AND ST. PAUL, located in 18th street, between Race and Summer, is decidedly the most prominent, not only in this city, but is the most magnificent church edifice in the United States.

THE METHODIST CHURCHES IN PHILADELPHIA, have 67 places of worship in the city, of which 10 are colored. *The first Church established* was the present "ST. GEORGE'S;" the next "EBENEZER," Second street, near Queen; and the Third, the "UNION." This society, second to none, in its influence in the country, probably includes more members than any other denomination of Christians. Their churches are generally plain but substantial edifices, built more for convenience than display.

There are seven HEBREW SYNAGOGUES in the city. The Synagogues in Philadelphia, like in all other places in the United States are respectively denominated "Spanish and Portuguese," and "German and Polish." This division does not arise from any difference either in their belief or ceremonial worship, but from the slight difference in the pronunciation of the Hebrew, and in some cases from the difference of the tone chant of some of their Psalms and prayers.

There are two INDEPENDENT OR CONGREGATIONAL CHURCHES in the city.

CHRISTIAN CHURCH.—There is but one of this denomination in Philadelphia, viz.: MOUNT ZION, Christian street, below Sixth.

THE BIBLE CHRISTIANS have a Church located on Third street, above Girard avenue.

THE DISCIPLES OF CHRIST—Twelfth street, below Melon.

CHURCH OF THE NEW TESTAMENT—Eleventh and Wood streets.

There are four MARINER'S CHURCHES in the city.

EVANGELICAL ASSOCIATION have five churches in the city. GERMAN BAPTISTS have two. THE UNITARIAN, one. THE UNIVERSALISTS, three. THE CONGREGATIONAL, three. FRENCH EVANGELIST'S, one; and the SPIRITUALISTS have two. The belief of the latter is, that after death, the spirit has an existence in *spheres* or *conditions*, and though invisible to mortal vision, are nevertheless immediately around us; and that (here lies the whole novelty of their faith) spirits of the departed can, and do, give positive evidence of their personal identity.

MISSIONARY BOARDS, &c.

American Board of Foreign Missions, No. 1334, Chestnut street.

American Sunday School Union is located in the fine granite building, No. 1122 Chestnut street.

Board of Foreign Missions of the General Synod of Reformed Presbyterian Church, Treasurer, S. G. Scott, No. 47 N. Third street.

Board of Foreign Missions of the United Presbyterian Church, T. B. Rich, Treasurer, Race street, below Sixteenth.

Board of Domestic Missions of the German Reformed Church, No. 493 N. Fourth street.

Board of Missions of the Diocese of Pennsylvania, No. 708 Walnut street.

Missionary Association for Seamen in the Port of Philadelphia.

Philadelphia City Missionary Society of the Lutheran Church.

Philadelphia Home Missionary Society, No. 1334 Chestnut street.

Presbyterian Board of Domestic Missions, No. 907 Arch street.

Protestant Episcopal Association for the promotion of christianity among the Jews.

The Home Missionary Society of the City of Philadelphia, No. 50 N. Seventh street.

Society of the Protestant Episcopal Church for the advancement of christianity in Pennsylvania. Rt. Rev. W. B. Stevens, President.

Young Men's Central Home Mission, Treasurer, No. 426 Market staeet.

Church Extension Society of the Methodist Episcopal Church, Rev. J. Castle, D. D., President, No. 1153 S. Fifteenth street.

Locust Street Mission Association, Locust street, above Ninth.

BIBLE AND TRACT PUBLICATION SOCIETIES.

Pennsylvania Bible Society, N. W. corner of Seventh and Walnut streets.

Philadelphia Bible Society, N. W. corner of Seventh and Walnut streets

Bible Association of Friends, No. 116 N. Fourth street.

American Sunday School Union, Publishing Department, No. 1122 Chestnut street.

American Baptist Publication Society, No. 530 Arch street.

American Tract Society, No. 1210 Chestnut street.

American New Tract Society, J. S. Siddal, Recording Secretary, No. 424 Library street.

Philadelphia Tract and Mission Society, No. 115 S. Seventh street.

Presbyterian Board of Publication, No. 821 Chestnut street.

Presbyterian Publication Committee, No. 1334 Chestnut street.

Tract Association of Friends, Depository, No. 304 Arch street.

Association of Friends for the Diffusion of Religious and Useful Knowledge, No. 109 N. 10th street.

Bishop White's Prayer Book Society, Agents, King & Baird, No. 607 Sansom street.

German Reformed Church Publication Board, No. 54 N. Sixth street.

Lutheran Publication Society, No. 42 N. Ninth street.

BOARDS OF EDUCATION.

Board of Education of the Presbyterian Church, No. 812 Chestnut street.

Pennsylvania Baptist Educational Society, No. 530 Arch street.

BENEVOLENT INSTITUTIONS, ETC.

THE PENNSYLVANIA HOSPITAL.—Pine and Spruce, Eighth and Ninth streets; entrance on Eighth street. This noble charity stands pre-eminent above all public establishments of the kind in this country; and in respect to the wisdom of its system, and excellence of its management, has no superior. The whole arrangement of both Hospital buildings, their perfect adaptation to their purpose, their neat, thoroughly ventilated, and scrupulously clean wards, arrest the attention of every visitor.

The Institution was chartered in 1751. The chartered body consists of all who have paid fifty dollars to the institution. These are called "Contributions." They elect the Managers and a Treasurer.

THE CITY HOSPITAL.—The patients are here under the care of a Medical Board, consisting of three physicians, three surgeons and two obstetricians, all contributors, who serve without compensation.

The Hospital, with its various appendant buildings, occupies the entire square between Eighth and Ninth and Spruce and Pine streets. Its principal Front is on the latter street. The central building is occupied by the Library, Apothecary Apartment, Steward's Rooms, Committee Rooms, &c. In the second story is a fine ward devoted as a lying-in hospital for married women. In the third story is an elegant amphitheatre for surgical operations and lectures. The east and west wings are divided into Medical and Surgical wards. The beautiful lawn in front of the centre buildings is ornamented with a statue of William Penn, in lead. The other branch of this institution is properly designated the

PENNSYLVANIA HOSPITAL FOR THE INSANE, and is located between Market street and Haverford road, in the Twenty-fourth Ward, on grounds embracing about one hundred acres. The corner-stone of this elegant building was laid on the 22d of June, 1836, and the house opened for reception of patients on the 1st of January, 1841. The Hospital is under the management of one physician.

Forty indigent patients are admitted on the charity list. The conditions are, that their cases shall offer a fair chance of cure. They are admitted for a period of six months; but if, at the expiration of that time, a reasonable expectation of cure remains, their stay may be extended. Our readers must remember that this is not an Asylum for the Insane, but an Hospital for their cure, if such is possible. Patients who are able to pay are also admitted. The rate of board, &c., is regulated by the means of the patients, and the accommodations required. This Hospital is divided into two departments, viz.: one for males and one for females.

A visit to the Hospital for the Insane, will amply repay any one who loves the beauties of nature, or the still greater beauties of beneficence in orderly, efficient, and extensive actions. Around the house are pleasure grounds, of finely diversified surface, adorned with flowers, shrubbery, and trees, and from various points commanding beautiful rural views. Neat isolated buildings are seen here and there, intended for the amusement or employment of the inmates, or for other purposes connected with their well-being. In the midst, the main edifice arises, imposing by its magnitude, and striking by its architectural character, arranged internally with every attention to healthfulness and comfort; where everything is exquisitely clean, everything in order, and where a refreshing atmosphere of kindness, cheerfulness, and all the gentler virtues, seem to breathe peacefully through hall, saloon, and chamber.

Visitors are admitted from 10 A. M., until sunset, on all week-days, except on Saturday afternoon. The Market street cars go direct to the Asylum.

WILLS HOSPITAL

For the Relief of the *Indigent Blind and Lame*, is one of the most beautifully located institutions in the city, being situated in Race street, between Eighteenth and Nineteenth streets, immediately opposite Logan Square, which, with the ample grounds attached to the Hospital, gives it all the advantages of a rural location.

This Hospital was founded by the late James Wills, of Philadelphia, who bequeathed to the city the sum of $108,396 65, for that purpose. The lot on which the Hospital is built, occupies the entire square, between Race and Cherry and Eighteenth and Nineteenth street.

This valuable Institution is under the direction of eighteen "Managers," elected by Councils for a period of three years; six members being elected annually.

Visitors can obtain admission by application to the Steward on the premises. Take the Race and Vine Street cars.

The Hospital of the Protestant Episcopal Church in Philadelphia, corner of Huntingdon and Front streets. This charity is another evidence of the liberality of the citizens of Philadelphia. The Hospital buildings, with the exception of Girard College, being the most noble range of buildings in the city. The style of architecture adopted, is the Norman Gothic, of which it is a beautiful example. It is supposed that this Hospital will surpass, when fully organized, in all respects, any similar institution in the world. The Hospital already has accommodations for two hundred patients, who are admitted without reference to their creed, color, or nation.

Charity Hospital, Buttonwood street, below Broad, is likewise established for the benefit of all citizens and strangers who require its aid.

St. Joseph's Hospital, Girard avenue and Seventeenth street, is another valuable institution, lately enlarged. It is under the charge of the "Sisters of Charity," and in a truly Christian spirit admits persons of every creed, nation and color.

The Children's Hospital of Philadelphia, Blight street, east of Broad, between Lombard and Pine streets, is intended for sick children, between the ages of ten and twelve years.

THE HOWARD HOSPITAL AND INFIRMARY OF INCURABLES, is located at Nos. 1518 and 1520 Lombard street, dispenses relief and assistance gratuitously to the poor.

PHILADELPHIA LYING-IN CHARITY AND NURSE SOCIETY, No 931 Race street, is intended to afford medical aid to indigent married women, at their own homes, and to furnish to such as require it, a competent nurse.

Incidental to these objects, attention is given to the careful training of suitable women for the responsible duties of the sick chamber, and a register of qualified nurses is kept at the establishment for public reference.

THE GERMAN HOSPITAL OF THE CITY OF PHILADELPHIA, 20th and Norris streets.

PRESTON RETREAT, OR LYING-IN HOSPITAL FOR INDIGENT MARRIED WOMEN, Hamilton, between 20th and 21st streets.

The facade of this elegant building is of Pennsylvania marble, and is ornamented with a beautiful Doric portico. The whole edifice is finished in the most thorough manner, and reflects great credit upon all concerned. The grounds around the hospital, add greatly to its appearance. They embrace the entire block from 20th to 21st street, and extend nearly to Spring Garden street. This charity was founded by the late Dr. Jonas Preston of this city.

ST. FRANCIS' HOSPITAL, Fourth street and Girard avenue.

THE JEWS' HOSPITAL, corner of Fisher and Westminster avenues.

Christ Church Hospital,

Belmont, 24th ward, owes its foundation to Dr. John Kearsley, formerly an eminent physician of this city, who bequeathed a considerable estate to the vestry of Christ Church, of which he was long an active and useful member, for this purpose.

Subsequent bequests and donations, among which was that of Mr. Joseph Dobbins of South Carolina, whose gift though not of as great value at the time of donation, as Dr. Kearsley's, (1798) has since, by increased value of real-estate, brought to the funds much larger revenues. The property bequeathed by Mr. Dobbins, consisted of five hundred pounds in cash, a lot on Fifth street adjoining the burial ground, and upon which spacious stores have been erected; and the entire square between Spruce and Pine and 18th and 19th streets, which after remaining unproductive for over seventy years, has been sold for one hundred and eighty thousand dollars, and is now covered with first class dwelling houses.

This gentleman lived fifteen years after making this donation. He died in Charleston, South Carolina, in 1804, at the age of seventy-one, leaving in addition to the above, as his will expresses it, "all his estate, real and personal, consisting of one hundred and twenty-six shares in the Bank of South Carolina, together with other property amounting to about six thousand dollars, to the poor and distressed widows supported by the bounty of Dr. Kearsley, in Christ Church Hospital."

Thus through the munificence of these two individuals, one of those useful and benevolent institutions that adorn our city, has been amply endowed. This institution was first opened at No. 111 Arch street. Subsequently a much more commodious building was erected on Cherry street, above Third. A proper application of the funds, demanded increased accommodations. These could not be obtained by an extension of the old building, owing to the active mercantile character of the neighborhood, and the consequent increased value of real estate. The managers very judiciously sought a location that would possess that quietness consonant to such an institution. This was obtained in Belmont, 24th Ward, where they have erected one of the most elegant buildings in Philadelphia, possessing accommodations for about one hundred inmates, viz.: "Poor and Distressed Women of the Episcopal Church."

The office of the Christ Church Hospital, is in Prune below 6th street.

THE CITY, OR MUNICIPAL, HOSPITAL, Lamb Tavern and Hart's lane roads, is under the control of the Board of Health.

THE CITY HOSPITAL, Blockley Alms House.

THE WOMEN'S HOSPITAL, North College avenue and 22d street.

THE CHILDREN'S HOSPITAL OF PHILADELPIA, Eleventh street, above Columbia avenue.

THE HOMEOPATHIC INFIRMARY, Coates and Eleventh streets.

The various medical colleges have also valuable hospital accommodations.

DISPENSARIES.

PHILADELPHIA DISPENSARY, No. 127 south Fifth street. This valuable charity was founded as early as 1786, with a view of furnishing gratuitous advice, surgical aid and medicines, to the poor.

In addition to this institution, there is *The Northern Dispensary*, No. 603 Spring Garden street; *Southern Dispensary*, No. 318 Shippen street; *Dispensary Department for the Poor*, Catharine street, above Seventh; *Homeopathic Infirmary*, S. E. corner of Coates and Eleventh streets; and *The Southern Homeopathic Dispensary*, No. 318 Shippen street.

In addition to these, we may mention that the various Medical Colleges dispense medical advice, aid and medicines gratuitously to the poor.

PENNSYLVANIA HOSPITAL.

ASYLUMS.

MAGDALEN ASYLUMS, OR "HOUSES OF MERCY." There are three of these associations in Philadelphia, viz.:—

The Magdalen Society, 21st and Race streets. The asylum is a spacious brick structure, surrounded by pleasant grounds. It was instituted in 1800, and chartered in 1802.

House of the Good Shepherd, Twenty-third street, between Sansom and Walnut streets. This institution is under charge of the Sisters of Charity.

The Rosine Association of Philadelphia, Rising Sun Village, on Germantown avenue.

PHILADELPHIA ORPHANS' SOCIETY ASYLUM— Race and 18th streets. This institution was formed in 1814, and incorporated in 1816. The building is of brick, constructed fire-proof to guard against the calamity of fire; a former building on this same site being destroyed by that element, with twenty-three of its little inmates, on the morning of January 22d, 1822.

Indigent Widows' and Single Women's Society of Philadelphia. This benevolent institution was founded in 1819. It is supported by contributions and bequests. The asylum is situated on Cherry street, east of 18th, immeditaely adjoining the Orphans' Asylum.

The Asylum for the Relief of Persons deprived of the use of their Reason.—This institution is beautifully located near Frankford, in the 23d Ward. It was founded in 1813, by the Society of Friends, with a view of affording to those afflicted with insanity, the domestic comforts usually found in a private family, combined with skillful moral and medical treatment.

The " Burd" Asylum of St. Stephen's Church—West Chester Road, above Cobb's creek. This is a magnificent endowment for the education of female orphans of the Episcopal Church.

The Penn Asylum for poor Widows and Single Women—Belgrade street, above Otis.

Asylum for Orphans and Widows of deceased Clergyman of the Lutheran Church—Germantown.

St. John's Asylum for Orphan Boys, is a noble institution, situated on Lancaster avenue, 24th Ward.

St. Joseph's Female Orphan Asylum—7th and Spruce streets.

St. Vincent's Orphan Asylum—at Tacony.

St. Ann's Widows' Asylum—Second street, below Christian.

German Reformed Orphan Asylum—situated in Bridesburg.

Colored Orphans' Asylum—Haverford road, 24th Ward.

HOMES FOR THE HOMELESS.

THE NORTHERN HOME FOR FRIENDLESS CHILDREN.—This institution, for the support and tuition of deserted or friendless children, under thirteen years of age, is located at the corner of Twenty-third and Brown streets. Another

CHILDREN'S HOME is located at the corner of Twelfth and Fitzwater streets. The object of both is to remove deserted children, under thirteen years of age, from the evil influences of the city, to the healthy and moral atmosphere of the country, during their minority.

THE WESTERN PROVIDENT HOME FOR CHILDREN—Logan and Venango streets, Twenty-fourth Ward, is another similar to the above.

THE TEMPORARY HOME ASSOCIATION OF PHILADELPHIA—No. 727 Filbert street, is intended to furnish a cheap and comfortable place of boarding to single women and children out of employment.

THE NEWS BOYS' AID SOCIETY—No. 221 Spruce street; instituted to provide lodgings and education for homeless and indigent boys engaged in selling newspapers.

INDUSTRIAL HOME FOR GIRLS—S. E. corner of Broad street and Columbia avenue. This institution was founded for the instruction of girls in the art of house-work and sewing, and thus prepare them for service in private families.

HOME FOR DESTITUTE COLORED CHILDREN—Maylandville, Twenty-fourth Ward. The object of this institution is similar to that of the

FOSTER HOME ASSOCIATION—Front and Huntingdon streets, a charity founded for providing a temporary home for the children of poor widows, &c., who are here fed, clothed, and educated at a small weekly charge. The house is entirely supported by the contributions of benevolent ladies, and the board of the children. It has no endowments.

ASSOCIATION FOR THE CARE OF COLORED CHILDREN—No. 708 Lombard street.

HOME FOR THE MORAL REFORM OF DESTITUTE CHILDREN—No. 708 Lombard street. In this house, destitute colored children are received, and trained for usefulness.

THE SOLDIER'S HOME, S. E. corner of 16th and Filbert streets, is a noble institution, supported by private and public contributions, and gives a home and shelter to all honorably discharged soldiers and sailors of the Union Army and Navy, who are unable, by reason of wounds or other disability, to support themselves.

GRANDOM FUND—Office, 811 Arch street. Part of this fund is employed in furnishing coal to deserving poor, at a reduced price, about half cost.

LUTHERAN HOME FOR ORPHANS—Germantown.

ST. VINCENT'S HOME FOR DESTITUTE INFANTS—Eighteenth and Wood streets.

CHURCH HOME FOR CHILDREN—N. E. corner of Twenty-second and Pine streets.

THE HOWARD INSTITUTION—No. 1612 Poplar street, is under the care of an association of ladies, principally belonging to "Friends."

YOUNG MEN'S HOME OF PHILADELPHIA—No. 1331 Filbert street.

In addition to these institutions, there are numerous Benevolent Associations founded for the relief and employment of the poor. Among them

THE FEMALE SOCIETY OF PHILADELPHIA—No. 112 North Seventh street, is one of the oldest in the city, having been instituted in 1793. Its object is to furnish employment, during the winter, at the House of Industry to aged women, and those with young children. A nursery department, well warmed rooms, and a comfortable dinner is provided, and a small compensation. The association also visit and attend the indigent sick.

THE PROVIDENT SOCIETY FOR EMPLOYING THE POOR—Prune, below Sixth street.

THE UNION BENEVOLENT ASSOCIATION—Office, South Seventh street, two doors north of Sansom.

THE WESTERN ASSOCIATION OF LADIES FOR THE RELIEF AND EMPLOYMENT OF THE POOR—Seventeenth street between Market and Chestnut streets.

The Northern Association of the City and County of Philadelphia, for the Relief and Employment of Poor Women—No. 702 Green street.

The Central Employment Association—S. E. corner of Green and Ninth streets.

The Philadelphia Society (for the Same Purpose)—Catharine street, between Seventh and Eighth.

The Home Missionary Society, Office, North street, near Fifth.

United Hebrew Relief Association, Central Station, Julianna Street Synagogue. The object of this Institution is to grant relief to the poor and helpless, and to support the aged, the infirm and the destitute of the Jewish faith.

Association of Friends for the relief of the suffering poor, No. 72 N. 4th street.

Female Association for the relief of the sick and infirm poor; French Benevolent Society; Swiss Benevolent Society; the various Hibernian Benevolent Societies; the numberless beneficial and mutual aid societies, connected with the various churches, trades and social orders, would fill a good sized volume with their names alone. In closing this chapter, we must not forget

The Philadelphia Association for the Relief of Disabled Firemen—Office, No. 34 North 5th street, because it is one of the most worthy charitable associations of the city, nor the

Soup Houses for supplying the poor, &c., of which there are eight in the city, viz.:—*The Central, The Philadelphia, The Northern, The Southwark, The Moyamensing, The Western, The Spring Garden,* and *The Kensington.* These houses are opened early in the winter, and are well supported by donations from the benevolent.

Other cities may boast of their "Royal Palaces" and magnificent works of art, but Philadelphia may well pride herself upon her Christian Benevolence.

MISCELLANEOUS ASSOCIATIONS.

A vast number of such associations abound in our city. We notice a few of the most prominent.

THE MASONIC ORDER
Is perhaps the most extensive and important of these organizations, both in numbers and character; but as *Secresy* is the obligation of the fraternity, we are unable to give definite information as to the objects or plan of operations of the order. Masons have ever been noted for their benevolence in all worthy enterprises. The head quarters of the order, is the

MASONIC HALL, Chestnut street, between 7th and 8th. This is the most spacious and ornate structure of the kind in the United States, the interior arrangements being in unison with its facade.

THE INDEPENDENT ORDER OF ODD FELLOWS— an organization similar in character to that of the Masons, have a handsome building on Sixth, below Cherry street, occupied as the headquarters of the order in this city. In addition to these principal, both Masons and Odd Fellows have other Lodge Rooms and Halls in and around the city.

THE SONS OF TEMPERANCE is a similar organization, in some respects, to the last named, but having for their specific object, the promotion of Temperance. There are now 24 "divisions" of the Sons of Temperance in this city, all in active operation.

OFFICE OF THE GRAND SCRIBE—No. 118 South Seventh street.

SOCIETIES OF ADOPTED CITIZENS AND FOREIGN RESIDENTS IN PHILADELPHIA.

There are several of these Societies organized as a bond of union, and to foster the recollections of their native land. They also extend their benevolence and assistance to those of their respective nationalities who may require their aid.

SOCIETY OF THE SONS OF ST. GEORGE.—W. H. Allen, Treasurer, No. 154 South Fourth street. ALBION SOCIETY.—J. Smedly, Agent, No. 211 Chestnut street. HIBERNIAN SOCIETY.—James Brown, Treasurer, No. 140 Walnut street. ST. ANDREW'S SOCIETY.—C. D. Ritchie, Secretary, No. 508 Walnut street. SCOT'S THISTLE SOCIETY.—John Booth, Secretary, No. 1630 Market street. FRENCH BENEVOLENT SOCIETY.— No. 36 South Fourth street. GERMAN SOCIETY, Hall No. 20 South Seventh street. The WELSH SOCIETY.—H. G. Jones, President, No.

133, South Fifth street. The SWISS BENEVOLENT SOCIETY—S. W. corner of Wood and Fourth streets.

CLUBS.

There are several clubs of gentlemen in Philadelphia. The most noted, however, is

THE UNION LEAGUE, whose object is to promote friendly intercourse among loyal people. The condition of membership is *unqualified loyalty to the Government of the United States.* The headquarters of the League is

THE UNION LEAGUE HOUSE,

S. W. corner of Broad and Sansom streets. This building, the first of the kind erected in Philadelphia, claims particular notice. The design of the structure is the French Renaissance, or, more strictly, the modern style of architecture. The facades are of fine pressed brick with granite and brown stone dressings, the basement story being of granite, while the steps and main entrance, together with the sills, architraves, and pediments of the windows are of brown stone. The angles of the building have also brown stone rustic quoins. The facade on Broad street is very elegant, being ornamented with a portico of four columns supporting a richly executed cornice. A balustrade, of fine execution and design, extends along the front of the spacious platform, which is approached by semicircular steps on the north and south extremities. The building is covered by a Mansard roof. A massive tower, in keeping with the general design of the main edifice, rises from the southwest angle. The main entrance leads into a spacious Hall extending the whole length of the building. This hall is fourteen feet wide, and has openings into beautifully ornamented and furnished rooms, respectively designated Parlor, Smoking Room, Publishing Room, Director's Room, Office, Private Dining Room, and Main Dining Saloon. The rear of this floor opens on a balcony, from which stairways lead to the tastefully ornamented garden.

A main stairway between the Smoking Room and Dining Saloon, lead to the second story, which contains a well furnished Library, a Reading Room, a Reception Room, and a grand Banquetting Saloon; these rooms are superbly furnished. The Basement contains a Billiard Room and a Supper Room, adjoining which is the Kitchen, Pantries, Store Rooms, &c.

Through the agency of this Association the following troops were put into the field during the late war: 1st Union League; 2d Union League, and 3d Union League Regiments; 4th Union League, or 183d Regiment Pa. Vols.;

5th Union League, or 196th Pa. Vols.; 6th Union League, or 198th Pa. Vols.; 7th Union League, or 213th Pa. Vols.; 8th Union League, or 214th Pa. Vols.; 9th Union League, or 215th Pa. Vols., together with the Gardner Battalion of Cavalry, comprising four full companies: the Dana Cavalry Troop, and a third battalion for the 198th Regiment Pa. Vols.; in all, 10,000 men.

The League has exerted also a wide spread influence during the same period, by the dissemination of loyal publications. "The Soldiers' Claim and Pension Agency," (designed to protect the unwary soldier from the swindling agencies of outside parties,) is mostly composed of members of this League. "The Supervisory Committee for Recruiting Colored Troops," was also composed of members of the League; and under their able management, eleven full regiments of colored troops were added to the National armies.

The League may well be congratulated for their eminent services to their country, as well as for their beautiful building, which adds so much to the street architecture of this city.

The National Union Club, No. 1105 Chestnut street, is a political association.

The Press Club is composed of gentlemen connected with the press. Rooms, No. 515 Chestnut street.

UNITED AMERICAN MECHANICS—There is an organization of this name having a Hall, N. E. corner of George and 4th streets, composed of, as its name implies, "American Mechanics." It is partly a beneficial society.

THE PENNSYLVANIA CLUB House, 1129 Chestnut street,

THE KEYSTONE CLUB, has no Hall or regular place of meeting. A large and influential class of citizens are, however, enrolled among its members. Colonel McCandless, is President of the club.

THE PHILADELPHIA CLUB HOUSE, 13th and Walnut streets, is a strictly private association.

In addition, there are several BOAT CLUBS' Club Houses, principally situated on the Schuylkill river, at the City Park.

Neat, tasty and safe boats are always on hire near these Boat Houses.

EXCHANGE AND BUSINESS ASSOCIATIONS.

Board of Brokers of the People's Exchange, No. 505 Chestnut street.

Butchers' and Melters' Association, Pennsylvania avenue, below 16th street.

Coal Exchange of Philadelphia, No. 205½ Walnut street.

Farmers' Hay and Market Exchange, 7th and Oxford streets.

Philadelphia Drug Exchange, No 17 S. Third street.   13

Foreign Consuls in Philadelphia.

Great Britain.—Charles Edward K. Kortright, No. 619 Walnut street.

France.—Francisque Charles Alphonse Lacathou de la Forrest, No. 524 Walnut street.

Austria.—S. Morris Waln, No. 128 S. Delaware avenue.

Republic of Costa Rica.—S. Morris Waln, No. 128 S. Delaware avenue.

Republic of Guatemala.—S. Morris Waln, No. 128 S. Delaware avenue.

Baden.—Clamor Frederick Hagedorn, No. 321 South Third street.

Bavaria.—Clamor Frederick Hagedorn, No. 321 South Third street.

Brunswick.—Clamor Frederick Hagedorn, No. 321 S. Third street.

Hesse-Cassel.—Clamor Frederick Hagedorn, No. 321 South Third street.

Hesse-Darmstadt.—Clamor Frederick Hagedorn, No. 321 South Third street.

Oldenburg.—Clamor Frederick Hagedorn, No. 321 South Third street.

Saxe-Coburg Gotha.—Clamor Frederick Hagedorn, No. 321 South Third Street.

Saxe-Weimar.—Clamor Frederick Hagedorn, No. 321 South Third street.

Bremen.—John T. Plate, No. 30 Bank street.

Hamburg.—John T. Plate, No. 30 Bank street.

Saxony.—John T. Plate, No. 30 Bank street.

Brazil.—Edward S. Sayres, No. 201 South Front street.

Denmark.—Edward S. Sayres, No. 201 South Front street.

Portugal.—Edward S. Sayres, No. 201 South Front street.

Sweden and Norway.—Edward S. Sayres, No. 101 South Front street.

Frankfort-on-the-Main.—John H. Harjes, No. 19½ Strawberry street.

Grand Duchy of Mechlenberg Schwerin.—John H. Harjes, No. 19½ Strawberry street.

Lubec.—John J. Harjes, No. 19½ Strawberry street.

Argentine Confederation.—J. Costas, No. 124 Walnut street.

Belgium.—G. E. Saurman, No. 1104 Chestnut street.

Buenos Ayres.—Nalbro Frazier, No. 105 Walnut street.

Chili.—Vacant.

Hayti.—Vacant.

Italy.—Viti M. Alonzo, No. 149 S. Front street.

Mexico.—Vacant.

Netherlands.—George K. Ziegler, No. 221 S. Fourth street.

Peru.—S. J. Christian, No. 141 North Water street.

Prussia.—C. C. Schottler, No. 30 Bank street.

Russia.—Henry Preant, No. 500 South Delaware avenue.

Spain.—Carlos de Rameaury Garcia, No. 925 Locust street.

Switzerland.—Rudolph Koradi, S. W. corner of Fourth and Wood streets.

Uruguay.—J. E. Bazley, No. 122 South Delaware avenue.

Oriental Republic of Uraguay.—J. E. Bazley, No. 122 South Delaware avenue.

Venezuela.—Leon de la Cova, No. 128 Walnut street.

Wurtemburg.—William Ludwig Kiderlin, No. 268 South Third street.

WALNUT STREET THEATRE.

PLACES OF AMUSEMENT.

Theatres.

In 1754, the first theatrical exhibitions in Philadelphia, were held in a store house, situated in Water street, near Pine. Subsequently a building was erected for the purpose, in South street. Popular prejudice was powerfully against this introduction of "European folly," so much so, as for several years to render the permanent establishment of Theatres doubtful. This opposition was to be expected from the religious and social habits of the population, which then found, and to a great extent do yet find, abundant amusement in social intercourse and home enjoyments. In 1791, the Theatre that lately stood on Chestnut street, west of Sixth, was erected. This place of amusement was long the favorite one in the city.

In 1809, "The Olympic," or present Walnut Street Theatre was built. This establishment intended and used many years for the representation of Pantomines, Olympic exercises, &c., was enlarged in 1813, and the house has since been in almost constant use as a regular theatre, for which the building, a commodious substantial and well designed structure, having been almost entirely rebuilt in 1865, is every way adapted.

At present, there are four regular theatrical establishments in this city, all of which are well attended.

ACADEMY OF MUSIC—Broad and Locust streets, was first opened to the public, January 26th, 1857. The building is of two stories, and has a front on Broad street of 140 feet, and extends 268 feet on Locust street. Its style of architecture is the "Romanesque."

The materials of the first story on Broad street, which forms its principal facade, is of a fine quality of brown stone. A line of the same material marks the height of this story on Locust street. The superior walls are of the finest pressed bricks. These walls are enormously thick and well put up. In this respect, the Academy may be regarded as one of the most substantial buildings in the country.

Five large doors extending along a projection of ninety feet, and a large window on its flanks, form the first story of the main front. Over these doors is a solid stone balcony, upon which open the windows of the second story.

On Locust street, there are thirteen similar openings to each story, five of them being doors in the first story, protected also by a stone balcony of like design to that on Broad street.

The entrance on Broad street, leads into a spacious hall, on the ends of which are the ticket offices. From this hall we pass into an elegant vestibule, 90 by 30 feet. Spacious flights of stairways, on the north and south extremities, lead to the upper tier of boxes. This vestibule is richly, yet chastely decorated.

Openings lead from this apartment into a lobby, thirteen feet wide, and extending along the east, north and south flanks of the auditorium, and has openings into each tier of boxes.

On the north side of the lobby, is the ladies' retiring room. A similar apartment for gentlemen is situated on the south side. The first tier of seats, is the range of boxes in the second story. This is called the "*Grand Dress Circle.*" The private boxes are in the rear of these, but are slightly elevated above the rest. This first tier communicates with a *Grand Saloon*, situated immediately over the vestibule. This room is 90 by 40 feet, with a ceiling 35 feet high. The decorations of this splendid saloon display refined taste. In this room the audience resort between the acts. It is also designed for banquets, balls, or concerts, for all of which it is well adapted.

The Parquette is traversed by two aisles. Over this space is the dome, which spans the whole auditorium. The dome is framed of strong iron work, covered. Its decorations are elaborately elegant.

Besides the Parquette and main Dress Circle, there are two other tiers of boxes. Altogether the auditorium will seat 3,500 persons.

The Proscenium is flanked by six massive columns, about 35 feet high. Between two of these, standing obliquely on each side, are the tiers of proscenium boxes, and over their entablature following the line of the columns, are gigantic figures, bending beneath the crowning entablature and pediment, from which springs the wide ellipse, spanning the stage in front of the curtain.

The house is lighted by a superb gilt and glass chandelier, 50 feet in circumference, depending from the centre of the dome, with 240 lights; these, with numerous beautiful brackets against the wall of each tier, shed brilliancy over the whole.

The Stage is the largest and best arranged in the United States. It presents a front of 50 feet, and extends back from the foot-lights, 93 feet.

MRS. JOHN DREW'S NEW ARCH STREET THEATRE.—Arch street, west of Sixth, is one of the most popular places of amusement in the city; the house having been lately rebuilt with all the modern improvements.

WALNUT STREET THEATRE—N. E. corner of

Walnut and Ninth streets. This place has been previously noticed.

NEW CHESTNUT STREET THEATRE—Chestnut street, west of Twelfth. This candidate for public favor, is situated in one of the most desirable locations in the city.

In addition to these Theatres there are numerous other places of amusement. Among them

FOX'S NEW AMERICAN THEATRE—Walnut street, above Eighth.

CARNCROSS AND DIXEY'S ETHIOPIAN OPERA HOUSE—Eleventh street, above Chestnut.

CONCERT HALL—Chestnut street, west of Twelfth. This is a beautiful room, where Concerts, Panoramos, Exhibitions, &c., are being constantly held.

PHILADELPHIA MUSEUM—No. 833 Market street.

ASSEMBLY BUILDINGS—Tenth and Chestnut streets.

MUSICAL FUND HALL—Locust street, between Eighth and Ninth. HANDEL AND HAYDN

HALL—Eighth and Spring Garden streets, together with numerous others in various parts of the city, constantly occupied for Concerts, Lectures, Balls, &c. Here we take occasion to warn the stranger against visiting any of the numerous "Concert Saloons," that abound in even our most prominent streets, where liquor is sold, the attraction of music, dancing, &c., being only a decoy to the worst of vices.

SKATING PARKS.

Union Skating Park—Fourth and Diamond streets.

Philadelphia Skating Park—Thirty-first and Walnut streets.

National Skating Park—Twenty-first street and Columbia avenue.

Keystone Skating Park—Third and Morris streets.

Bushnell's Skating Park—Broad street, above Columbia avenue.

Eastwick Skating Park—Gray's Ferry Road.

Central Skating Park—Fifteenth and Wallace streets.

West Philadelphia Base Ball and Skating Park—Forty-first street, north of Lancaster avenue.

PUBLIC SQUARES, PARKS, AND GROUNDS.

Of all the improvements, which we have witnessed in Philadelphia, the planting and opening of public squares and parks, is the most beautiful and salutary. We never pass through or near them, and see the happy and healthy beings who people them, enjoying the pure air and the fresh verdure, the music of birds, the rustling of the rich foliage, and all the other sights and sounds of rural life; women and children free from annoyance or the apprehension of it, though unguarded and unprotected, without feeling doubly contented with our country, and the place of our birth and residence.

THE STATE HOUSE, OR INDEPENDENCE SQUARE, was purchased by the Provincial Assembly in 1782, for the erection of State buildings, &c. It was subsequently purchased from the State by the city, with the *proviso*, that it should ever be maintained as an open walk, free to the public. This Square is celebrated as the scene of many of the most important events in the history of the nation. It was here, at a public assembly, that John Adams nominated George Washington as Commander-in-Chief of the American armies; and it was in this Square that The Independence of the Colonies was first proclaimed to the world.

WASHINGTON SQUARE, opposite State House, or Independence Square, was formerly the "Pottersfield," a place where the unknown dead, or the children of poverty were buried, without a stone or memorial to mark the end of their wanderings or troubles. What thoughts and memories does this beautiful Square conjure up of the unfortunate dead, that lie beneath the pleasant shade of its spreading trees. This was one of the original Squares, designed by William Penn, to adorn his city.

THE FRANKLIN SQUARE—bounded by Sixth, Race, Vine and Franklin streets, was also used at one time as a common burying ground. It is now one of the most beautiful spots in the city, having an elegant fountain in its centre.

Why not erect a monument in this square to the memory of him whose name it bears?

LOGAN SQUARE—bounded by Race, Vine, 18th and 19th streets, is another of the original squares laid out in the plan of the city. In 1864 the "Sanitary Fair" rendered this square a scene of social enjoyment and benevolence, that will be long remembered by the thousands who participated in it.

RITTENHOUSE SQUARE—bounded by Walnut,

Locust, 18th and 19th streets. The neighborhood of these last two squares is occupied by some of the most elegant private residences in the city.

THE PENN SQUARES—Broad and Market streets, were designed by William Penn for public buildings, for the accommodation of city offices, nor could a more suitable location be obtained for such purposes.

JEFFERSON SQUARE—between 3d and 4th streets, and Washington avenue and Federal street.

NORRIS SQUARE—in the northern part of the city, is bounded by Howard, Hancock and Diamond streets, on its east, west, and south fronts, and by Susquehanna avenue on the north front, was given by Isaac Parker Norris, to the public.

SCHACKAMAXON SQUARE.—This is a small plot of ground situated at the junction of Laurel and Beach streets. It was formerly the site of a market house. It has been neatly enclosed and planted with trees and shrubs. This was devised to the public by William Masters.

HUNTING PARK—York Road and Nicetown Lane. This new Park was the gift of several citizens. It contains 43 acres, and a plan from designs of Mr. John Saunders, for its improvement, has been adopted. When finished, it will contain the finest avenue of Tulip Poplars in the Middle States.

PARADE GROUND—is situated on the northwest side of the County Prison.

FOX SQUARE—between West Gaul, and Tioga streets.

GERMANTOWN SQUARE—between Courtland and Wyoming streets.

FAIRMOUNT, OR CITY PARK, extends along the entire eastern front of the Schuylkill River, from the Suspension, or Wire Bridge, to a point north of the Girard Avenue Bridge. It embraces the Fairmount Water Works, the former "Pratt's Garden," "Sedgley Park," and the "Schuylkill Water Works."

The scenery along the shores of the Schuylkill river, from the dam to the Columbia Bridge, is exceedingly beautiful. The east bank above the Park, presenting for the most part a wild and picturesque appearance, while the west shore abounds in lovely landscapes. Immediately opposite the City Park, on the west shore, is "Solitude," the once country seat of the Penn family; to the north of which, on the opposite side of Girard Avenue Bridge, is "Egglesfield," another country seat of olden days. Both of these charming places are fast going into ruin, and if not rescued by the city, will soon be among the things that were. Still further north, "Sweet Brier" meets the eye, situated on one of the most desirable locations on the river.

Adjoining this last, is *Landsdowne Park*, formerly "Landsdowne Manor." There are few spots in the vicinity of Philadelphia, more beautiful than this. The Manor House was originally erected by John Penn, but the estate subsequently became the property of the Bingham family. Here, Washington, at one time, established his headquarters. 40th street forms the western, and Hancock avenue the southern front of this Park.

Point Breeze Park and Race Course— is situated on the Penrose Ferry Road, near the Ferry Bridge. The property belongs to an association of gentlemen.

ENTRANCE TO LAUREL HILL CEMETERY.

CEMETERIES.

The Swedes Church Burying Ground, was the first place of interment in the city of Philadelphia. A dense and active population now occupy this ancient spot so that the visitor can form no conception of its picturesque appearance, "when far below the city;" it stood in the midst of a majestic growth of forest trees that extended to the river.

The Friends' Burial Ground, Arch and Fourth streets, is also an ancient place of interment, having been dedicated to this purpose in 1683. The first person buried here was Governor's Lloyd's wife. William Penn addressed the mourners at her grave.

Christ Church Burial Ground, was the third place of this kind opened in the city. This cemetery, situated on the corner of Arch and Fifth streets, was for many years the fashionable burial place. In it, repose the remains of the celebrated Benjamin Franklin, and Deborah, his wife.

Generally the old church burial grounds, of which there are many yet remaining in the city, are devoid of ornament, and possess no interest to the traveller. The number of interments in them are rapidly diminishing.

THE MUTUAL BURYING GROUND, Washington avenue, above Ninth street, though boasting of no architectural beauty or rural adornments, was the first cemetery established in the United States, subject to no clerical denomination. It was opened for interments in 1824.

LAUREL HILL CEMETERY, Ridge avenue, near the "Falls," Schuylkill river, is beautifully situated on the banks of the river, and is easy of access at all times by the passenger railway cars *via* the Ridge avenue, and by the small steamboats, running from Fairmount, during the summer months.

WOODLAND CEMETERY, Darby road, opposite the city, about one mile south of Market street. The grounds of this cemetery, formerly the country seat of a private family, are beautifully picturesque, and the views through the glades and avenues are unsurpassed for sweetness and repose. A drive through this cemetery will prove interesting. The views of the city, of the river Schuylkill, and of the Delaware, in the far horizon, are very fine.

Ronaldson Cemetery, situated at Ninth and Shippen streets.

Machpelah Cemetery, Washington avenue, from Tenth to Eleventh streets.

Lebanon Cemetery, Passyunk road, west of Broad street.

Philadelphia Cemetery, Passyunk road, west of Broad street.

Philanthropic Cemetery, Passyunk road, below County Prison.

Lafayette Cemetery, block from Ninth to Tenth, and from Federal to Wharton streets.

Cathedral Cemetery, Lancaster turnpike, 24th Ward.

Glenwood Cemetery, Ridge road and Islington lane.

Mount Vernon Cemetery, Ridge Road, opposite Laurel Hill.

The Monument Cemetery, Broad street, above Montgomery avenue.

The Odd Fellows' Cemetery, situated on 24th street and Islington lane.

The American Mechanics' Cemetery, Islington lane and 21st street.

St. Mary's Cemetery, Buck Road, below County Prison.

Olive Cemetery, Lancaster avenue, 24th Ward.

Mount Moriah Cemetery, Darby turnpike, 3 miles from the Market Street Bridge.

Mount Sinai Cemetery, Bridesburg.

Friends' Cemetery, West Chester road.

Fair Hill Cemetery, Germantown turnpike and Cambria street.

Hebrew Cemetery, Frankford.

Cedar Hill Cemetery, Frankford.

Leverington Cemetery, Roxborough.

Beth-el-Emeth Cemetery, Fisher's avenue and Market street.

In rural beauty and picturesque appearance the cemeteries of Philadelphia are, perhaps, unrivalled by any similar places in the world. All of them have been instituted since 1824. The adornments of these grounds, and their monuments, many of which being specimens of high art, are evidences of the refined taste of our citizens. They are really places of interest and beauty, perfect flower gardens, where trees, shrubs and flowers of every hue and variety, throw a delicious shade around. In such places, when the birds are singing, and the trees and plants present their verdure, the grave loses its gloom, and death is robbed of half its terror.

The Potters' Field, or City Burial Ground, is situated on Hart's Lane and Lamb Tavern Road. The unreclaimed dead under charge of the Coroner, the poor from the County Prison, Eastern Penitentiary, and Pennsylvania Hospital, find here their last resting place. The poor from the Alms House, are intered in ground attached to that Institution.

HOTELS

CONTINENTAL HOTEL, S. E. corner of Ninth and Chestnut streets. This building is one of the best adapted in the country for hotel purposes. The facade on Chestnut street, is of Pictou sandstone, that on Ninth street is of pressed brick, dressed with massive quoins, sill courses, and window heads of stone; the whole crowned with a rich and ornamental cornice. The erection and completion of this hotel is due to a few public spirited citizens. For the convenience of strangers, a Book and Periodical Depot is attached to the house, where choice seats to all places of amusement in the city can be had, together with Railroad Tickets, &c. This cabinet of conveniences is in the main hall, adjoining the office.

THE GIRARD HOUSE, Chestnut street, opposite the Continental is also a fine building.

THE LA PIERRE HOUSE, Broad street, below Chestnut, occupies one of the best locations in the city. It presents every feature of a private mansion, with all the elegancies and enjoyments of the most popular hotels.

MERCHANTS' HOTEL, Fourth street, below Arch. This favorite resort of merchants, is one of the most popular Houses in the city.

American Hotel, Chestnut, between Fifth and Sixth streets.

Washington House, Chestnut street, above Seventh.

Bingham House, Eleventh and Market streets.

The Union, Arch street, above Third.

The Bald Eagle, No. 416 North Third street.

The Barley Sheaf, No. 257 North Second street.

St. Lawrence Hotel, No. 1018 Chestnut street.

Allegheny House, No. 814 Market street.

Arch Street House, corner Delaware avenue and Arch street.

Markoe House, Chestnut street, above Ninth.

St. Charles' Hotel, Third street, below Arch.

Mount Vernon Hotel, Second, above Arch street.

Ridgeway House, No. 1 Market street.

Western Hotel, No. 826 Market street.

Walnut street House, corner of Walnut street and Delaware avenue.

THE CENTRAL POST OFFICE, Chestnut Street.

WM. F. WARBURTON,
Fashionable Hatter,
430 CHESTNUT STREET, below Fifth,
PHILADELPHIA.

ADJOINING NEW POST OFFICE.

NEWSPAPERS.

The first newspaper published in Philadelphia, was the "Weekly Mercury," an eight by twelve inch single sheet, printed two columns on a side. The circulation of this paper extended through New York, New Jersey, Maryland, Virginia, and even to Boston. The first number is dated December 22d, 1719, and is almost entirely filled with news from Europe. The first general advertisement is in the second issue. It states "that a mulatto boy, named Johnny, aged twenty-two years, and of a *very white complexion*," ran away from his master. Five pounds was the reward offered for Johnny. The first regular business notice states, "that very good seasoned pine boards, and cedar shingles are to be sold by Charles Read, opposite Thomas Master's store, at the corner of Front and Market streets, where any person can have cocoa ground, or be supplied with right good chocolate cheap." In the issues of the first six months we find an occasional "*extra*" or double sheet; one of which contains an account of "An extraordinary revolution in the Province of South Carolina, in which the people overthrew the authority of the 'Proprietors' by turning out their Governor and his Council, and electing one More as their chief, in the name of King George." We allude to this early pioneer of a power that has since exerted such an influence on the destiny of this country, that our readers may compare it with the paper, supplied to them each day, teeming with news, not only from Europe but from all parts of the world. In their columns, the reader can also find every kind of business fully advertised. Indeed, at the present day, no practical man expects to succeed without availing himself of this widespread means of publicity. The following is a correct list of

THE PRESS OF PHILADELPHIA IN 1870.

NEWSPAPERS.

DAILY.

North American and United States Gazette, No. 132 S. 3d street.

Public Ledger, S. W. corner of 6th and Chestnut streets.

The Day, N. W. corner of 6th and Chestnut streets.

The Philadelphia Inquirer, No. 304 Chestnut street.
The Daily Press, S. W. corner of 7th and Chestnut streets.
Daily Evening Bulletin, No. 607 Chestnut street.
Daily Evening Telegraph, No. 108 S. 3d street.
Philadelphia Free Press, (German,) 418 N. 4th street.
Philadelphia Democrat, 614 Chestnut street.
The Age, No. 14 S. 7th street.
North American and United States Gazette, No. 132 S. 3d street.
The Star, 34 S. 7th street.
The Morning Post, 34 S. 7th street.

WEEKLY.

Sunday Dispatch, No. 152 S. 3d street.
Sunday Mercury, No. 152 S. 3d street.
Sunday Transcript, N. W. corner of 7th and Chestnut streets.
Sunday Morning Times, No. 136 S. 3d street.
Saturday Night, S. W. corner of 8th and Locust streets.
Germantown Telegraph, Main street, Germantown.
Saturday Evening Post, No. 319 Walnut street.
Weekly North American, No. 132 S. 3d street.

Weekly Press, S. W. corner of 7th and Chestnut streets.

Fitzgerald's City Item, No. 112 S. 3d street.

Republican Flag, No. 418 N. 4th street.

Sunday Blatt, No. 418 N. 4th street.

New World, No. 465 N. 3d street.

United States Journal, No. 310 Chestnut street.

United States Rail-Road and Mining Register, No. 423 Walnut street.

Commercial Lists, No. 241 Dock street.

Vereingte Staaten Zeitung, No. 465 N. 3d street.

Fincher's Trades' Review, No. 441 Chestnut street.

Legal Intelligencer, No. 607 Sansom street.

Legal and Insurance Reporter, No. 703 Walnut street.

National Merchant, No. 409 Chestnut street.

Reformoite Kirchenzeitung, No. 54 N. 6th street.

Friends' Review, No. 109 N. 10th street.

Friends' Intelligencer, No. 131 N. 7th street.

German Reformed Messenger, No. 52 N. 6th street.

Long's Monthly Children's Letters, No. 1210 Chestnut street.

American Presbyterian, No. 1334 Chestnut street.

Banner of the Covenant, No. 1334 Chestnut street.

Anti-Slavery Standard, No. 5 S. 5th street.

Christian Recorder, No. 619 Pine street.

Catholic Herald, No. 310 Chestnut street.
Episcopal Recorder, No. 237 Dock street.
Lutheran and Missionary, No. 42 N. 9th street.
National Baptist, No. 530 Arch street.
Sunday School Times, No. 614 Arch street.
Presbyterian Standard, No. 108 S. 4th street.
The Presbyterian, No. 1334 Chestnut street.
The Friend, 116 N. 4th.

PERIODICALS.

Godey's Lady's Book, No. 537 Chestnut street.
Peterson's Ladies National Magazine, No. 306 Chestnut street.
Lady's Friend, No. 319 Walnut street.
Arthur's Home Magazine, No. 323 Walnut street.
Gardiner's Monthly, No. 23 N. 6th street.
Home and Foreign Record, No. 821 Chestnut street.
The Child's World, No. 1122 Chestnut street.
Little Pilgrim, No. 319 Walnut street.
Guardian, No. 52 N. 6th street.
Young Reaper, No. 530 Arch street.
Sabbath School Visitor, No. 821 Chestnut street.
The Occident, No. 1227 Walnut street.
Temperance Standard, Frankford.

Lammer Herte, Bridesburg.

Kirchenhcund, S. W. corner 4th and Wood streets.

Clark's School Visitor, No. 1308 Chestnut street.

American Educational, No. 512 Arch street.

American Exchange and Review, No. 521 Chestnut street.

American Journal of Medical Sciences, No. 710 Sansom street.

American Journal of Pharmacy, N. E. corner of 7th and Market streets.

American Law Register, No. 131 S. 5th street.

American Botschafter. No. 1210 Chestnut street

Biblical Repertory, and Princeton Review, No. 821 Chestnut street.

Dental Cosmos, No. 528 Arch street.

Eclectal Medical Journal, N. E. corner of 6th and Callowhill streets.

Evangelical Repository, No. 1023 Race street.

Herald of Health, No. 25 S. 10th street.

Imlay and Bicknell's Bank Note Reporter, No 45 S. 3d street.

Peterson's Counterfeit Detector, No. 306 Chestnut street.

Journal of the Academy of Natural Sciences, N. W. corner of Broad and Sansom streets.

Journal of the Franklin Institute, No. 15 S. 7th street.

Colonization Herald, No. 609 Chestnut street.

Lutheran Sunday School Herald, No. 43 N. 9th street.

Medical News and Library, No. 710 Sansom street.

Medical and Surgical Reporter, No. 115 S. 7th street.

Phrenological Journal, No. 25 S. 10th street.

Presbyterian Historical Almanac, No. 133 S. 18th street.

Proceedings of the Academy of Natural Sciences, N. W. corner of Broad and Sansom streets.

Sabbath School Treasury, No. 54 N. 6th street.

Sunday School World, No. 1122 Chestnut street.

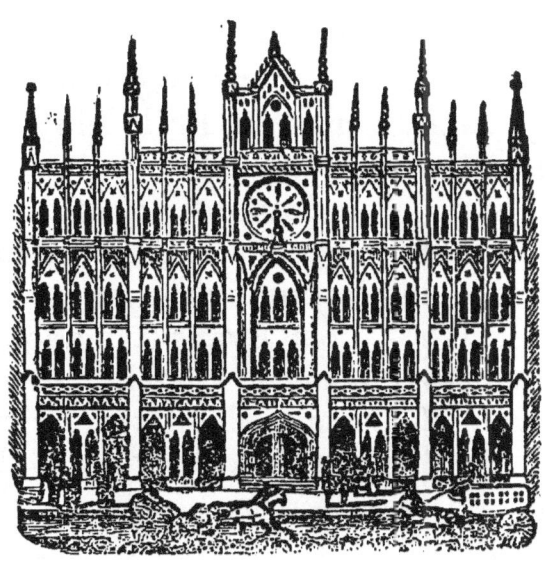

MASONIC HALL, Chestnut Street between Seventh and Eighth Streets.

RAIL ROADS.

It was an important era in the history of civilization when steam was first applied to the purpose of travel.

Without this agent, a large portion of our country, now teeming with its millions of inhabitants, would yet be a wilderness; and the sites of cities now flourishing with busy populations, engaged in trade and manufacture, would be still in the solitude of nature. The vast stores of wealth contained in the mountains and valleys of our own noble state, would have remained buried in her bosom, and the productive industry contingent upon these stores, making so many happy homes in Philadelphia, would have remained undeveloped.

The history of the introduction of the railway system in Pennsylvania alone, would make an exceedingly interesting work of itself. We might relate how poor Evans struggled against the prejudices of his age, when he proposed the application of steam to land travel, and how such men as Stephen Girard, *ridiculed* the idea, denominating it "Utopian;" that none of all the monied interest of Philadelphia were found to give him the required aid of *one thousand dollars* to prove the practicability of the plan. The opportunity passed, and other lands and people had the honor of adapting steam to the purposes of land travel. We might relate the discouragements of the projectors of the "Columbia Railroad," the first constructed in the State, even after the plan had been adopted elsewhere, and its immense value fully demonstrated, but our limits will not permit.

It is only within the last fifteen or twenty years, that the vast importance of the railway system became manifest to our citizens. Since then, it has received a cordial support, and a magnificent network of these roads, diverging from Philadelphia, intersect, not only our own State, but all parts of the country.

In the following notices of railroads diverging from Philadelphia, we omit Time-table, owing to the changes continually made in them.

PENNSYLVANIA CENTRAL RAILROAD—Director's Office, is the rich and elegant brown stone building, No. 234 to 238 South Third street, below Walnut.

PASSENGER DEPOT—Thirty-first and Market streets. This road connects Philadelphia with the West, Northwest, South and Southwestern States. At Pittsburg it unites with lines leading to Cleveland, Detroit, Chicago, Millwauke, and intermediate cities and towns in North-western Ohio, Indiana, and Illinois. From Chicago, the connection continues *via* the Alton and Chicago Railroad to St. Louis, intersecting that vast network of railways running through the rich and fertile States of Illinois and Indiana. At Pittsburg, it also forms a union with the Columbus and Cincinnati Railroad, which, with its various branch roads, leads through Central and Southern Ohio, Indiana and Illinois, as well as those running through Kentucky, Tennessee, and Southwest.

In its route through Pennsylvania, it forms connections with the York and Wrightsville Railroad; The Northern Central Railroad; The Cumberland Valley Railroad; The Lebanon Valley Railroad; The Schuylkill and Susquehanna Railroad; The Huntingdon and Broad Top Railroad; The Tyrone and Clearfield Railroad; The Hollidaysburg Branch Railway; The Ebensburg and Cresson Railroad, and The Indiana Branch Railway.

The construction of this magnificent road will ever remain a monument to the enterprise of its founders, and the skill of its engineers.

DISTANCES AND STATIONS FROM PHILADELPHIA TO PITTSBURG.

STATIONS.	MILES.	STATIONS.	MILES.
Philadelphia,		Athensville,	9
Hestonville,	4	White Hall,	11
Libertyville,	7	Villa Nova,	13

HAND-BOOK IN PHILADELPHIA.

STATIONS.	MILES.	STATIONS.	MILES.
Morgan's Corner,	14	Manyunk,	184
Eagle,	17	Newton Hamilton,	189
Paoli,	21	Mount Union,	192
Steamboat,	26	Mapleton,	196
Oakland,	29	Mill Creek,	199
West Chester Intersection.		Huntingdon,	204
Int. Chester Valley R.	33	Petersburg,	211
Downingtown,	34	Barre,	214
Gallagherville,	35	Spruce Creek,	217
Caln,	38	Birmingham,	221
Coatsville, (Midway)	40	Tyrone,	223
Chandlers,	43	Tipton's,	227
Parkesburg,	45	Fostoria,	230
Penningtonville,	48	Bell's Mill,	232
Christiana,	49	Altoona,	238
Gap,	52	Kittanning Point,	244
Kinzers,	55	Gallitzin,	250
Lemon Place,	58	Cresson,	253
Gordonsville,	59	Lilly's,	256
Bird in Hand,	62	Portage,	261
Lancaster,	69	Wilmore,	263
Dillerville,	71	Summer Hill,	266
Landisville,	78	Viaduct,	269
Mount Joy,	82	Conemaugh,	274
Elizabethtown,	88	Johnstown,	277
Middletown,	97	Conemaugh Furnace,	285
Highspire,	101	Nineveh,	286
Harrisburg,	107	New Florence,	290
Rockville,	112	Lockport,	295
Cove,	117	Bolivar,	297
Duncannon,	121	Blairsville Inter.,	301
Aqueduct,	124	Hillside,	306
Baileysburg,	130	Derry,	309
Newport,	134	St. Clair,	311
Millerstown,	140	Latrobe,	314
Thompsontown,	145	Beatty's,	317
Mexico,	151	George's,	321
Perrysville,	153	Greensburg,	324
Mifflin,	156	Radebaugh's	326
Lewistown,	168	Grapeville,	328
Andersons,	175	Manor,	331
McVeytown,	179	Irwin's,	333

STATIONS.	MILES.	STATIONS.	MILES.
Larimer's,	335	Swissvale,	347
Stewart's,	338	Wilkinsburg,	348
Turtle Creek,	342	Homewood,	349
Brinton's,	343	Liberty,	350
Braddock's,	345	Pittsburgh,	355

PHILADELPHIA AND READING RAILROAD— General Office of this Company, No. 227 South Fourth Street.

PASSENGER AND MERCHANDISE STATION, corner of Broad and Callowhill streets.—COAL WHARVES, at Richmond, on the Delaware river.

This road runs through the Schuylkill Valley, a distance of 112 miles to Harrisburg, connecting the great anthracite coal fields with tide water. Its branches and connections, both numerous and of immense value, are as follows: At Norristown it connects with the Philadelphia, Germantown and Norristown Railroad, and Chester Valley Railroad; at Reading, with the Lebanon Valley Railroad, 54 miles to Harrisburg, connecting there with the Pennsylvania Central Railroad, the Northern Central Railway and the Cumberland Valley Railroad; at Reading it also connects with the East Pennsylvania Railroad, which is finished, 36 miles to Allentown, (and soon to be completed 16 miles further to Easton), where it connects with the Lehigh Valley Railroad to Easton, and thence by the Central Railroad of

New Jersey, or Morris and Essex Railroad, through the thickly populated and beautiful hilly country of Northern New Jersey to New York. At Easton, connection is likewise made with the Belvidere Delaware Railroad, running through the valley of the Delaware River from Trenton to the Delaware Water Gap; also, at Reading with the Reading and Columbia Railway through the rich farming region of Berks and Lancaster counties, past the celebrated Ephrata and Litiz watering places to Columbia and Lancaster. At Port Clinton the Little Schuylkill Railroad joins this road, a line of itself some 28 miles long, and running through the eastern end of the Schuylkill coal field, past Tamaqua to the junction of the Catawissa Railroad, now leased by the Atlantic and Great Western Railroad, which expects in a few months to perfect its connections to the west, so as to make a continuous through route of the same guage as the Reading Road (4 feet 8½ inches) from Philadelphia to Chicago and Cincinanti, thus conforming to the general system of Western Railroads.

At Auburn, the Schuylkill and Susquehanna Rail Road from Rockville, a point 5 miles above Harrisburg on the Susquehanna River, comes in, passing along a most lonely valley which borders the whole southern side of the coal field, and by several feeders pours the products of the mines along their route into the main road. At Schuylkill Haven, a most wonderful display of the "Black Diamonds" are to be seen. At this point the Mine Hill Rail Road terminates; a road whose main stem is only about 30 miles long, and yet has some 130 miles of track, and carries about three millions of tons of coal in a year.

From Schuylkill Haven to Pottsville, there are numerous feeders or lateral railroads, ramifying North, East, and West, making a perfect network of iron. The total length of single track owned and controlled by the Reading Railroad, does not fall much short of 1000 miles. The number of locomotives is about 275, total number of coal cars, 13,500; of all other kinds, 2,900. Transportation last year, 3,100,000 tons of coal, and 1,100,000 tons of freight.

PHILADELPHIA AND READING RAILROAD.

STATIONS.	MILES.	STATIONS.	MILES.
Philadelphia,	0	Leesport,	66
Conshohocken,	13½	Mohrsville,	68½
Norristown,	17	Shoemakersville,	70
Port Kennedy,	21½	Hamburg,	75
Valley Forge,	23½	Pt. Clinton,	78
Phœnixville,	27½	Auburn,	83
Royer's Bridge,	32	Orwigsburg,	86
Limerick,	34	Schuylkill Haven,	85
Pottstown,	40	Mount Carbon,	92
Douglassville,	44½	Pottsville,	93
Birdsboro',	49	Harrisburg,	112
Reading,	58		

New York Lines.

Camden and Amboy Railroad, *via* **South Amboy**—Depot, Walnut street wharf.

Passengers by this line take the ferry at the depot to Camden, thence by cars to South Amboy; thence by steamboat to New York, landing at the foot of Barclay street. This route affords the traveller a view of New York Bay and Harbor, Staten Island, Brooklyn, Jersey City, and the National Forts, altogether forming a scene unsurpassed by any other in the world.

STATIONS.	MILES.	STATIONS.	MILES.
Philadelphia,		Newton,	34
Camden,		Windsor,	37
Palmyra,	8	Highstown,	40
Riverton,	9	Cranberry,	43
Delanco,	13	Prospect Plains,	45
Beverly,	15	Jamesburg,	48
Burlington,	19	Spottswood,	51
Florence,	23	South River,	54
Bordentown,	27	South Amboy,	61
Trenton,	33	New York,	90

Camden and Amboy Railroad from Philadelphia to New York, *via* **Camden and Jersey City.**

Passengers leave Walnut street wharf by ferry to Camden, thence by cars to Jersey City and way stations.

STATIONS.	MILES.	STATIONS.	MILES.
Camden,		Princeton,	37½
Palmyra,	8	Kingston,	44¼
Riverton,	9	New Brunswick,	53½
Delanco,	13	Metuchin,	63
Beverly,	15	Rahway,	68
Barlington,	18	Elizabeth,	73
Florence,	23	Newark,	78½
Bordentown,	27	Jersey City,	86
Trenton,	33	New York,	88

FOR NEW YORK BY THE PHILADELPHIA AND TRENTON RAILROAD, from Kensington Depot, Front and Harrison streets. Passengers will take the Second and Third street, or Fifth and Sixth Street cars.

STATIONS.	MILES.	STATIONS.	MILES.
Philadelphia,		New Brunswick,	53½
Tacony,	6	Metuchin,	63
Cornwell's,	12½	Rahway,	68
Bristol,	17	Elizabeth,	73
Trenton,	28	Newark,	78½
Princeton,	37½	Jersey City,	8
Kingston,	44¼	New York,	8

RARITAN AND DELAWARE BAY RAILRO. OR NEW YORK.—Passengers take the Fer t Vine street wharf to Cooper's Ferry, Camde rom whence trains leave twice daily (Sunda xcepted) for New York and the followin way stations. A fine view of New York Bay, Staten Island, Sandy Hook, Coney Island, Long Island, &c., is had by this route from Port Monmouth.

STATIONS.	MILES.	STATIONS.	MILES.
Camden,	1	Shark River,	78
Jackson,	20	Junction,	84
Atsion,	29	Edontown,	85
Harris,	38	Shrewsbury,	
Shamong,	41	Oceanport,	86
Lebanon,	44	Red Bank,	87
Woodmansie,	46	Branch Port,	88
Whiting's Mills,	53	Long Branch,	89
Ridgeway,	59	Port Monmouth,	92
Bergen Iron Works,	67	Steamboat to	
Squankum,	73	New York,	113

CAMDEN AND ATLANTIC RAILROAD.—Trains for Atlantic City and Way Stations, leave Vine street Ferry daily.

STATIONS.	MILES.	STATIONS.	MILES.
Cooper's Point,	1	Winslow,	$27\frac{3}{4}$
Haddonfield,	$7\frac{3}{4}$	Hammonton,	$30\frac{1}{4}$
Ashland,	11	Da Costa,	$32\frac{3}{4}$
White Horse,	$12\frac{1}{4}$	Elwood,	$37\frac{1}{2}$
Long-a-coming,	$17\frac{1}{2}$	Egg Harbour,	$41\frac{3}{4}$
Jackson,	20	Patkouk,	48
Waterford,	$23\frac{3}{4}$	Absecom,	$53\frac{1}{4}$
Spring Garden,	$25\frac{1}{4}$	Atlantic,	$60\frac{1}{4}$

WEST JERSEY RAILROAD FOR CAPE MAY AND WAY STATIONS.—Take Ferry at Market street Wharf to Camden.

STATIONS.	MILES.	STATIONS.	MILES
Philadelphia,		Marlboro',	$15\frac{1}{4}$
Camden,		Glassboro',	18
Gloucester,	$3\frac{3}{4}$	Fislerville,	$21\frac{1}{4}$
Westville,	$5\frac{1}{2}$	Franklinville,	$24\frac{1}{4}$
Woodbury,	$8\frac{1}{3}$	Cranes,	$26\frac{1}{2}$
Mantua,	$11\frac{3}{4}$	Malaga,	$28\frac{1}{4}$
Barnsboro',	$13\frac{1}{3}$	Lake,	$29\frac{1}{2}$

STATIONS.	MILES.	STATIONS.	MILES.
Forest Grove,	$33\frac{1}{2}$	Seaville,	$62\frac{1}{4}$
Vineland,	35	Swain,	$66\frac{3}{4}$
Millville,	40	C. May C. House,	$69\frac{3}{4}$
Manumuskin,	$46\frac{3}{4}$	Millerton,	$73\frac{1}{4}$
Belleplain,	$53\frac{1}{2}$	Rio Grande,	$75\frac{1}{2}$
Woodbine,	$56\frac{3}{4}$	Bennetts,	$78\frac{1}{2}$
Mt. Pleasant,	$59\frac{1}{4}$	Cape May,	$81\frac{1}{2}$

PHILADELPHIA, WILMINGTON, AND BALTIMORE RAILROAD—Depot, Broad street and Washington avenue.

This is the great Southern route through Washington to the Southern States. The Depot of the Company is the finest structure of the kind in the city. The Thirteenth and Fifteenth Street, and the Union, Seventh and Ninth Street lines of Horse Cars connect with this depot.

STATIONS.	MILES.	STATIONS.	MILES.
Philadelphia		North East,	52
Bell Road,	6	Charlestown,	55
Lazaretto,	11	Principio,	58
Chester,	14	Perryville,	61
Thurlow,	16	Havre de Grace,	62
Linwood,	18	Aberdeen,	67
Claymont,	20	Perryman's,	71
Holly Oak,	22	Edgewood,	74
Bellevue,	23	Magnolia,	79
Wilmington,	28	Harewood,	81
Newport,	32	Chase's,	83
Stanton,	34	Stemmer's Run,	89
Newark,	40	Baltimore,	98
Elkton,	46		

PHILADELPHIA, GERMANTOWN AND NORRISTOWN RAIL ROAD.—Depot, 9th and Green streets.

GERMANTOWN BRANCH.

STATIONS.	MILES.	STATIONS.	MILES.
Tioga,		Washington,	
Wayne,		Mount Pleasant,	
Fisher's		Mount Airy,	
Duy's,		Mermaid,	
Shoemaker,		Hospital,	
Church,		Graver's,	
Germantown,	5	Chestnut Hill,	
High Street,			

NORRISTOWN BRANCH.

STATIONS.	MILES.	STATIONS.	MILES.
Falls,		Lafayette,	
School Lane,		Spring Mill,	8
Wissahickon,		Conshohocken,	12
Manayunk,		Potts,	
Green Tree,		Mogees,	
Soap Stone,		Norristown,	17

WEST CHESTER AND PHILADELPHIA RAIL ROAD, *via* MEDIA—Office and Depot, 31st and Market streets, south side.

STATIONS.	MILES.	STATIONS.	MILES.
Philadelphia,		Media,	14
Gray's Lane,	3	Glen Riddle,	16½
Church Lane,	4	Lenm,	17
Darby Road,	5	Pennelton,	18
Kelleyville,	7	Darlington,	19
Clifton,	8	Glen Mills,	20
Spring Hill,	9	Cheyney's Shops,	22
Newton's,	10	Street Road,	24
West Dale,	11	Hemphill's,	26
Wallingford,	12½	West Chester,	28

Connects at Pennelton, with the Philadelphia and Baltimore Central Railroad.

Connects at West Chester, with West Chester Railroad, which connects near Paoli with Pennsylvania Central.

PENNSYLVANIA AND ERIE RAIL ROAD—traverses the northern counties of Pennsylvania.

It is now leased by the Pennsylvania Central Railroad.

Passengers take cars at the Depot, 31st and Market streets.

STATIONS.	MILES.	STATIONS.	MILES.
Harrisburg,	107	Hemlock,	317
Sunbury,	163	St. Mary's,	323
Northumberland,	165	Ridgway,	332
Lewisburg,	172	Johnsonburg,	341
Catawissa Junction	175	Wilcox,	247
Milton,	176	Kane,	356
Watsontown,	180	Wetmore,	361
Dewart,	183	Sheffield,	371
Montgomery,	187	Pattonia,	378
Muncy,	191	Ottis,	383
Montoursville,	198	Warren,	385
Williamsport,	203	Irvine,	390
Elmira Junction,	204	Youngsville,	393
Newbury,	205	Pittsfield,	396
Susquehanna,	209	Garland,	400
Jersey Shore,	215	Spring Creek,	406
Wayne,	223	Columbus,	411
Lock Haven,	228	Corry,	413
Farrandsville,	233	Lovell's,	417
Wetham,	243	Concord,	419
North Point,	252	Union,	424
Renovo,	255	LeBoeuf,	428
Keating,	267	Waterford,	432
Sinnemahoning,	280	Jackson's,	438
Driftwood,	283	Langdon's,	442
Sterling,	292	Belle Valley,	444
Cameron,	296	Erie,	451
Emporium,	301		

NORTH PENNSYLVANIA RAIL ROAD.—Office, No. 407 Walnut street. Depot, Berks and America streets.

STATIONS.	MILES.	STATIONS.	MILES
Philadelphia,		Gwynedd,	18
Tioga street,	2¼	North Wales,	20
Fisher's Lane	4	Landsdale,	22
Green Lane,	5	Line Lexington,	24½
Oak Lane,	6	Hatfield,	25
City Line,	6¼	White Hall,	27
Old York Road,	7¼	Souders,	27½
Chelton Hills,	8¼	New Britain,	29
Jenkintown,	8½	Sellersville,	31¼
Abington,	9¾	Doylestown,	32
Edge Hill,	10¾	Quakertown,	38
Sandy Run,	12½	Coopersburg,	43½
Fort Washington,	13½	Centre Valley,	46
Wissahickon,	15	Hellerton,	50
Pennllyn,	16½	Bethlehem,	54

street

CUSTOM HOUSE.

CITY PASSENGER RAIL ROADS.

The passenger railway system of Philadelphia is perfect. It traverses almost every considerable street of the city, and in many cases extends for miles beyond, in the country and suburban towns. The cars are neat, clean, and commodious, and their conductors gentlemanly and attentive. Only one improvement more is wanting to render the system all that can be desired, and that is the substitution of steam for horse power.

SECOND AND THIRD STREET RAILWAY—Runs from Bridesburg, *down Second street* to the Navy Yard, and back, *up Third street.*

GREEN AND COATES STREET RAILWAY— From Fairmount, *via* 22d and Green streets to Fourth, *down Fourth* to Walnut, up Walnut to Eighth, *up Eighth* to Coates, *out Coates* (passing the Eastern Penitentiary,) to Fairmount. Also *down Fourth* to Dickerson street, out Dickerson to Eighth, *up Eighth* to Coates, &c. *These cars are painted Green,*

GERMANTOWN PASSENGER RAILWAY, runs from Mount Airy, down *Germantown Road* to Fourth street, *down Fourth* to Walnut, *out Walnut* to Eighth street, *up Eighth* to Germantown Road; also *down Fourth* to Dickerson street, out Dickerson street to Eighth, *up Eighth* to Germantown Road, *out Germantown Road* to Mount Airy. *The cars of this Company are painted yellow.*

FRANKFORD AND SOUTHWARK, OR FIFTH AND SIXTH STREET RAILWAY.—These cars run from Frankford, *down Sixth* to Morris street in the First Ward, thence *down Morris* to Fifth street, and return *up Fifth* to Frankford.

UNION—*Richmond Branch, Brown Cars*—Broad and Prime to Christian, thence *down to Ninth* street *up* to Spring Garden, *down to Seventh,* up to Oxford, down to Fourth, up to Susquehanna avenue; along Susquehanna and Emerald to York street, *down York to Thompson street* and the Depot of the Company. Returning, along Thompson to Marlborough, Belgrade and Frankford Road to Master street, *up Master* to Franklin, *down Franklin* and Seventh to Passyunk Road along to Ellsworth, *out Ellsworth* to Broad and the Baltimore Depot.

Fairmount Branch, Yellow Cars—From Navy Yard by Front street and Wharton street to Ninth, *up Ninth* to Spring Garden, thence to Twenty-third, *out Twenty-third* to Brown street, out to Park. Back on Brown to Twenty-Third along to Wallace, *down Wallace* to Franklin to Seventh, *down Seventh* to Federal, and *down Federal* to Navy Yard gate.

TENTH AND ELEVENTH STREET, OR CITIZEN'S PASSENGER RAILWAY.—The cars of this road run from Columbia avenue, *down Tenth street* to Moyamensing Prison, returning *up Eleventh* street to Columbia avenue.

THIRTEENTH AND FIFTEENTH STREET RAILWAY.—Run from Columbia avenue, *down Thirteenth* street to the Philadelphia, Wilmington, and Baltimore Railroad Depot, returning *up Fifteenth* street to the place of starting.

SEVENTEENTH AND NINETEENTH STREET RAILWAY—from Master street *down Seventeenth* to Washington avenue, returning *up Nineteenth* street, passing Girard College, to the place of starting.

RICHMOND AND SCHUYLKILL, OR GIRARD AVENUE RAILWAY—*Double Track.*—These cars run from Richmond, in the Nineteenth Ward, and by Girard avenue to (passing Girard College) Girard Avenue Bridge, over which it passes into West Philadelphia.

RIDGE AVENUE—*Double Track*—from Second street out Arch to Ninth street, *up Ninth* to Ridge avenue, thence out Ridge avenue to Girard College.

MANAYUNK—*Ridge avenue*—runs from *connection* with Ridge Avenue Railway, out Ridge Road, passing the Glenwood, Mount Vernon, and Laurel Hill Cemeteries; the Falls of Schuylkill, and the Wissahickon to Manayunk.

FAIRMOUNT AND EXCHANGE, OR RACE AND VINE STREET RAILWAY—Runs from Exchange *up* Third to Vine street, *up Vine* to Fairmount, returning *down* Race street, to place of beginning.

HESTONVILLE, MANTUA, AND FAIRMOUNT RAILWAY—*Double Track*—Runs from Front *out Callowhill* street to Wire Bridge at Fairmount, also from Wire Bridge, through West Philadelphia, to Hestonville.

WEST PHILADELPHIA MARKET STREET RAILWAY—*Double Track*—Runs from Front street, out Market to west end of Twenty-fourth Ward. This is the nearest route to the Pennsylvania Hospital for the Insane (Kirkbride's) and also to the Burd Orphan Asylum.

DARBY PASSENGER RAILWAY—Runs from Market street, West Philadelphia, by Darby Road to Darby. These cars pass the Alms House and the Woodlands Cemetery.

PHILADELPHIA CITY PASSENGER RAILWAY, CHESTNUT AND WALNUT STREETS.—The cars of this line run from Front street, *up Walnut* to Twenty-second street, and *back* by Chestnut street.

PHILADELPHIA AND GRAY'S FERRY, SPRUCE AND PINE STREETS.—Runs from Exchange *down Dock* to Second street, down Second to Pine, *up Pine* and *back* by Spruce street. The Naval

Asylum, United States Arsenal, and Gray's Ferry Bridge, can be reached by these cars.

PHILADELPHIA AND OLNEY RAILWAY—Runs from Lehigh avenue to the village of Olney in the Twenty-Second Ward, commences at Sixth and Diamond streets.

NORTH PHILADELPHIA RAILWAY—Runs from the terminus of Tenth and Eleventh Street Road, Columbia avenue, to Germantown *via* Broad street, Tioga street, and Plank Road.

DELAWARE COUNTY, BLOCKLEY AND MERION—Runs from connection with West Philadelphia Railway, to the Spread Eagle Hotel, in the Twenty-fourth Ward.

LOMBARD AND SOUTH STREET RAILWAY—Runs *out* South street, from Front to Chippewa street, up Chippewa to Lombard, *down* Lombard to Front.

NAVY YARD. Cars of Union Line run to the gate.

FERRIES.

West Jersey Ferry, from lower side of Market street to Market street, Camden.

Camden and Philadelphia Ferry, from the upper side of Market street to Federal street, Camden.

Camden Ferry, from the upper side of South street to Kaign's Point, Camden.

Cooper's Point Ferry, from Vine street to Cooper's Point, Camden.

Gloucester Ferry, from South street to Gloucester, New Jersey.

Red Bank Ferry, from South street to Red Bank, New Jersey.

STEAMBOATS PLYING ON THE DELAWARE.

Ariel, leaves Chestnut street wharf for Chester, Marcus Hook, and Wilmington.

Major Reybold, leaves Arch street wharf for Chester, Penn's Grove, New Castle, Delaware City, and Salem.

Edwin Forrest, leaves Arch street wharf for Beverly, Burlington, Bristol, Florence, Fieldsbrough and Trenton.

John A. Warner, leaves Arch street wharf for Riverton, Torresdale, Andalusia, Beverly, Burlington, and Bristol.

Barclay, leaves first wharf below Arch street, for Progress, Delanco, Delta Grove, Bridgebrough, Irish Wharf, Bailey's Landing, and Centerton.

Trenton, Walnut street Wharf for Tacony, Torresdale, Beverly, College Wharf, and Burlington.

Rancocas, first wharf below Arch street, for Bridgeport.

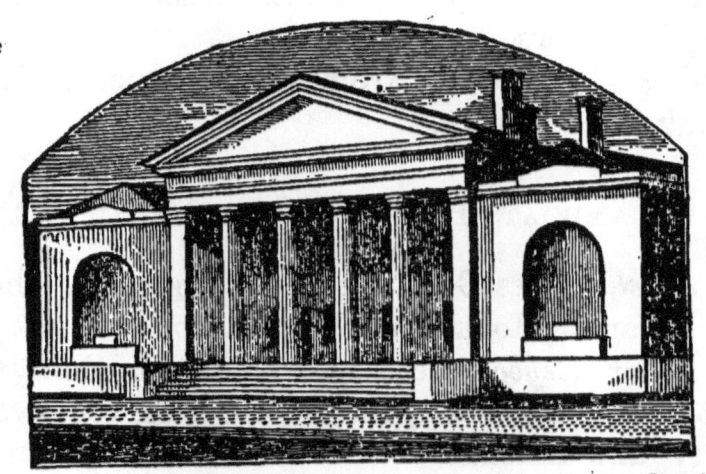

DEAF AND DUMB ASYLUM, N. W. cor. Broad and Pine Streets.

RATES OF FARE, ETC., OF HACKNEY COACHES.

Any distance not exceeding one mile, fifty cents, and for every additional passenger twenty-five cents.

Any distance more than a mile, and not exceeding two miles, seventy-five cents, and for every additional passenger twenty-five cents.

Any distance over two miles, for every such additional mile, or part of a mile, the sum of twenty-five cents in addition to the sum of seventy-five cents for the first two miles, and for every additional passenger twenty-five cents.

For the use of a hackney carriage by the hour, with one or two passengers, with the privilege of going from place to place, and stopping as often as may be required, *one dollar per hour.*

In all cases, where the hiring of a hackney carriage is not at the time specified to be by the hour, it shall be deemed to be by the mile; but in case the distance shall be more than four miles, the rate to be charged for each additional mile shall be twelve and a half cents for each passenger.

For children between two and fourteen years of age, half price is only to be charged; and for children under two years of age, no charge is to be made.

Every driver or owner of a hackney carriage shall carry, transport, and convey in, and upon his carriage, in addition to the persons therein, one trunk, valise, saddle-bag, carpet-bag, portmanteau or box, if requested so to do, for each passenger, without charge or compensation therefor; but for every trunk or other such articles above named, more than one for each passenger, he shall be entitled to demand and receive the sum of six cents.

Chestnut street, south to Prime, about 1 mile.
Chestnut " north to Brown, " 1 mile.
Delaware river to Twelfth street, " 1 mile.
Delaware river to Schuylkill river " 2 miles.

Camden and Amboy Depot, Walnut street wharf, to Trenton Depot, about 2 miles.

Camden and Amboy Depot, Walnut street wharf, to Baltimore Depot, Broad and Prime streets, 2 miles.

In case of disputes about fares go the Mayor's Office.

TELEGRAPH COMPANIES.

American, No. 105 South Third street.
United States, Third and Chestnut streets.
Western Union, No. 105 South Third street.
Peoples, No. 111 Chestnut street.
Philadelphia, Reading, and Pottsville, No. 225 South Fourth street.
Philadelphia and Wilkesbarre, No. 105 South Third street.
Susquehanna River, and North and West Branch, No. 225 South Fourth street.

FIRST PRESBYTERIAN CHURCH.

LOCATIONS OF OFFICES OF THE UNITED STATES ASSESSORS AND COLLECTORS

IN PHILADELPHIA.

1st *District*—Assessor, No. 271 South Third street.
" Collector, No. 419 Chestnut street.
2d *District*—Assessor, S. E. corner Eighth and Walnut streets.
" Collector, Jayne's Building, Dock, bel. 3d street.
3d *District*—Assessor, No. 924 North Third street.
" Collector, S. W. corner Third and Willow streets.
4th *District*—Assessor, Spring Garden Hall, 13th and Spring Garden streets.
" Collector, Spring Garden Hall, 13th and Spring Garden streets.
5th *District*—Assessor, Germantown.
" Collector, Doylestown.

Revenue Agency,
No. 427 Chestnut street.

COMMERCE OF PHILADELPHIA.

The foreign exports through the Philadelphia Custom House for the fiscal year ending June 30th, 1865, amounted to $10,978,603. The imports were $7,154,804.

The real commerce of the city cannot be ascertained, inasmuch as the greater portion of the foreign trade of Philadelphia, is done through New York. An idea of its extent may be inferred, when we state that millions of tons of merchandise are transported annually over the railroads and canals, between New York and Philadelphia.

Many Philadelphia Merchants also store their imports in bonded warehouses in New York, until sold, when they are transported direct to the purchaser. Thus, vast quantities of goods and merchandise, really imported by Philadelphia Houses, never reach this city. Stranger still than this, merchants send their exports over to New York for shipment; not only flour, grain, &c., but coal, iron, and lumber, all of which can be shipped direct from Philadelphia, at less expense than from New York.

The only reason for this is *lack of enterprise* among commercial men in this city. A change is coming however. A few years more, and immense docks, equal, if not surpassing those of London and Liverpool, will line the Delaware at, and below its junction with the Schuylkill, where vessels can receive their freight direct, by railway, from the great West, and the rich fields of our State. Here, too, will be immense elevators and depots for the reception of produce and trade, where all the various lines of railroads from the North, South and West will centre. At this, the true harbor of Philadelphia, the largest ships of the world can ride in safety, the ingress and egress being open winter and summer, high or low tide.

UNITED STATES MINT, Chestnut Street, east of Broad.

PHILADELPHIA, THE MANUFACTURING METROPOLIS OF THE UNION.

The hydrographic basin of every river in Pennsylvania is a source of iron supply. In the valley of the Schuylkill, within fifteen miles of Philadelphia, furnaces are in blast making pig-iron from ores near by. From the eastern counties of the State, by rail and water routes, home made iron of every kind and quality, and in any quantity can be delivered in this city at a less cost in transportation, than to any other market. Hence iron is sold cheaper in Philadelphia, than in any other city.

Coal is brought to Philadelphia direct from the mines, over six carrying routes, three railroads and three canals. The coal fields are nearer, and the transportation cheaper to Philadelphia, than to any other seaboard city. Of the coal annually brought to it, over one million tons are forwarded to New York. This could not be done if the difference in favor of Philadelphia were not equal to the cost of transportation from it to New York. Immense quantities of this article is also shipped hence to Boston and other eastern markets.

By this unlimited and economical supply of

raw material, Philadelphia has some of the most extensive manufacturing establishments in the world. There are now employed in iron and steel manufactories in this city alone, over 12,000 men, whose annual productions exceed $17,000,000. In the vicinity, within a few miles, there are thirty-four forges, foundries and rolling mills, employing over 3000 men, and producing nearly $5,000,000 annually. There are seven shipping foundries, and iron ship building establishments; two for manufacturing heavy machinists' tools, iron plates, drills, &c.; three forges for ship shafts, and heavy plate and axles; twelve rolling mills, bar, plate, and sheet; two heavy ordnance foundries; two manufactories of small arms; one for heavy wrought ordnance; three for shot and shell; fifty-three for steam engines and general machinery; four locomotives, axles and car wheels; and twenty-five general foundries and building foundries.

The capacity of these works, is enormous. Of the two manufactories of small arms, one of them is only surpassed in its capacity of turning out work, by those at Springfield.

There are ninety-two cotton mills, ninety-six mills on mixed cotton and woollen goods, forty-seven mills employed on woollen goods, thirty-two mills on cotton yarns, cotton laps, waddings

&c., cotton webbing and taps, one hundred and two on woollen and cotton hosiery, and one hundred and twenty-four manufacturing carpets, principally ingrain. While there are three silk spinning mills, and thirty-one establishments engaged on silk ornamental goods, principally trimmings, fringes, tassels, ribbons, &c. There are ten silk printing and dye works; twelve print and dye works; thirty-five dyers of yarn and twists; three dry goods finishing establishments, and three hair cloth establishments—in short, there are no less than six hundred and thirty-one establishments in the city, manufacturing textile fabrics, all operated by either steam or water power, but principally steam. Every branch of industry found in other manufacturing centres is represented in this city.

The local markets of Philadelphia have long been celebrated for their profusion and cheapness, and the extent of the highly cultivated country from which they are supplied.

Grain, flour, beef, pork, &c., can be laid down from Chicago, or any other great exporting point of the west, cheaper at Philadelphia than at New York. Such stores are, and always have been cheaper to purchase in this market, for European or tropical export, than in any other on the Atlantic coast. The distance traversed from the great producing districts of the west to Philadelphia, is 90 miles less than to New York. In all that relates to the supply of raw material, the cost and supply of labor, the maintenance of men and the abundance and cheapness of provisions, Philadelphia is truly without a rival.

Philadelphia has long been celebrated for the superiority of the dwellings occupied by workmen of all classes. Hundred of streets are built up with neat and comfortable brick houses, supplied with both water and gas, the rent of which is from $10 to $20 per month. Similar dwellings are unknown in New York. Workingmen in that city, occupy apartments in those tenement houses, that reflect so much upon its sanitary condition. This superiority, both in cost and comfort of buildings for the residence of men in all grades of employment, is the pride of Philadelphia, and the admiration of all strangers.

SWEETMOUTH.

TREGO'S TEABERRY TOOTHWASH

Is the most Pleasant, Cheapest and Best Dentifrice Extant.

SOLE PROPRIETOR AND MANUFACTURER OF

TREGO'S TEABERRY TOOTHWASH,
A. M. WILSON, Druggist,
9th and Filbert Streets,
PHILADELPHIA.

Ask your Druggist for it. Take no other.

COPY YOUR LETTERS IN THE

PENN LETTER BOOK!!

WITHOUT THE USE OF COPYING PRESS OR WATER.

This is the greatest *Time, Labor, and Money Saving Invention of the Age,* and is rapidly growing into favor wherever introduced, as its *Simplicity* and *Convenience* recommend it to all. It is only necessary to place the written letter under the copying leaf, and rub with the hand.

Every one will acknowledge the importance of keeping a fac-simile copy of every business letter written, and the PENN LETTER BOOK brings the means of doing so within the reach of ALL. Full directions for use accompany each book.

PRICE, FOR BOOK AND INK, COMPLETE, $2.25, AND UPWARD.

Call and see it, or send for full descriptive Circulars to

P. GARRETT & CO., Sole Proprietors,
702 *Chestnut Street,* (2d *Story,*) *Philadelphia,*
or, 128 *South Clark St., Chicago.*

Also, "100 Choice Selections," Nos. 1, 2 and 3,

Containing the best new things for Declamations, Recitations, School-reading, etc., and combining Brilliant Oratory, Thrilling Sentiment and Sparkling Humor.

Price for either number, pamphlet edition, 30 cents; cloth bound, 75 cents.

Every speaker should have these books, and a copy of "EXCELSIOR DIALOGUES," new edition. Price $1.25.

B. J. WILLIAMS & SONS,

No. 16 North Sixth St.,

PHILADELPHIA.

LARGEST MANUFACTURERS OF

Venetian Blinds

AND

Window Shades,

SELL AT THE LOWEST PRICES.

Blinds Repaired,
      Store Shades,
           Trimmings,
                Fixtures.

PLAIN SHADES OF ALL KINDS,

CURTAIN CORNICES,

Picture Tassels, Cord Bell Pulls, &c.

The Weekly Press.

This first General News, Family, and Agricultural Journal has more than doubled its circulation since the campaign, and now circulates extensively, especially through the Middle States and the West. Its Political Department is under special charge of HON. JOHN W. FORNEY, and its Agricultural Department—the best in America—is edited by THOMAS MEEHAN, of the *Gardeners' Monthly*. Terms: $2.00 per annum; Fifteen copies for $10.00. It has the latest markets of every description, fresh to the hour of going to press.

CIRCULATION, - - 16,000.

An excellent Advertising Medium.

FOR TERMS, ADDRESS,

M. T. WOLF,

ADVERTISING AGENT FOR "THE WEEKLY PRESS,"

S. W. cor. Seventh and Chestnut Streets.

PHILADELPHIA.

d

THE LEADING
DEMOCRATIC PAPER
IN PENNSYLVANIA.

The Only Democratic Morning Journal (in English) published in Philadelphia.

TERMS OF SUBSCRIPTION:

Daily, $8 per year;   Weekly, $1.50 per year.

Offices, 14 & 16 South Seventh St., Philad'a.

WELSH & ROBB, Proprietors.

www.ingramcontent.com/pod-product-compliance
Lightning Source LLC
Chambersburg PA
CBHW020920230426
43666CB00008B/1518